Law of Realization

What "The Secret*" Don't Tell You

*and other books, movies, and programs

Jim Britt
Anthony Hernandez

THE LAW OF REALIZATION

Jim Britt
Anthony Hernandez

Cover art by Don Ellis Aguillo
www.donaguillo.com

Master Key Productions, Inc.
10556 Combie Road, Suite 6205
Auburn, CA 9560n

Britt, Jim
Hernandez, Anthony
The Law of Realization
978-0-9662171-1-7 (paperback)
978-0-9662171-2-4 (Amazon® Kindle®)
978-0-9662171-3-1 (EPUB)

Dedication

Jim Britt: This book is dedicated to the open-minded individual who seeks to know the truth.

Anthony Hernandez: This book is dedicated to my partner Jennifer and my son Logan who give me so many reasons to realize joy and love.

* * *

Foreword

Just about every day I meet people who feel they are not reaching their full potential. I ask these people what steps they took to create their ideal life and I often hear this answer:

"I set unattainable goals and chased my dreams ever since."

It feels awful chasing something that is always just out of reach. Real progress requires leadership. Being a leader allows me to achieve my goals. It makes me responsible for everything in my life.

Most potential leaders never take charge because they fear failure. This fear comes from remembering past failures or lessons that drive us to hold ourselves back. Letting go of fear, stress, anxiety and other negativity are essential. This flushes the negative energy you are carrying.

Having a positive mindset is the key to building wealth and achieving your goals. Changing your mindset is like putting on different glasses that highlight different areas of what you see. This shows you opportunities you may have missed before. A positive mindset helps you achieve your goals by opening your mind and reducing or even eliminating your fears.

Mindset opens the door but action takes you through that door into the land of opportunity. You have to take action everyday. Track your progress and manage your resources. Get help from your team. You will need the right team to help you and manage your resources.

Manage your success like a business. Life itself is the most important business there is! Never overextend yourself. Work is good. Progress is great. Get plenty of sleep and exercise to keep mind and body in top condition. Find ways to get more done with less and pocket the time you save. There is no such thing as "work" time and "personal" time. There is only time, and time is energy.

The Law of Realization will help show you how to use your energy to overcome your own limitations. Anthony's science will fascinate you. Jim's simple principles will empower you. *The Law of Realization* is a must read!

Loral Langemeier
Bestselling Author of the three-part *The Millionaire Maker* series
Featured in *The Secret*
www.LiveOutLoud.com

Introduction

The Law of Attraction lies at the heart of most of today's self-help programs thanks to movies such as *What the Bleep Do We Know?* and best-selling books such as *The Secret, The Law of Attraction: The Basics of the Teachings of Abraham*, and *The Law of Attraction: The Science of Attracting More of What You Want and Less of What You Don't.* The self-help experts who subscribe to the Law of Attraction say that quantum physics, neurology (brain science), and other disciplines prove that the Law of Attraction is just as much a natural law as the law of gravity. Is this true?

Yes and no. Much of science is wide open to interpretation and scientists disagree about a great many things. This includes the science behind the Law of Attraction. For example, just about all scientists agree about the data provided by quantum physics but many disagree about how to interpret that data. We know the math. We don't know for sure what that math is trying to tell us.

Some interpretations are more "far out" than others. This does not necessarily make them wrong but the mainstream scientific community regards "far out" scientists with skepticism. Self-help experts who rely on findings provided by "far out" scientists often find themselves being looked at with suspicion and regarded as hucksters and snake-oil peddlers. Most mainstream scientists dismiss the Law of Attraction as anything from wishful thinking to outright fraud. This is unfortunate because most self-help experts are good and honest people who are on a noble mission to help others lead better lives.

We live in a wonderful universe in which just about anything we can imagine is possible. Yes, you can go from rags to riches, from sadness to joy, and can have just about anything you want. Yes, you can "manifest" all this. The Law of Attraction is very real.

The catch is that the Law of Attraction is both very subtle and very limited. The odds of you being able to attract and manifest what you want are so low that you may as well not even try. That's the bad news.

Don't lose hope! The good news is that you really do have the power to change your life anytime you want. You already use this power all the time whether you know it or not. Everything in your life is a complete success because there is no such thing as failure. The only question is whether the success you experience is the success you want. If not, that means that you need to learn how to use your power more effectively. This is the crucial ingredient that many self-help programs based on the Law of Attraction miss altogether.

We need to be very clear that it is absolutely not our intention to attack or disparage any self-help program based on the Law of Attraction. Most self-help programs contain valuable lessons and insights that can help people improve their lives. Many of them need only minor updates to be compatible with current scientific understanding. It's a bit like lifting up a gorgeous house to repair the foundation and then setting it back down stronger and better than ever before.

You will learn about quantum physics in this book. You will also gain new insights into what is happening inside your head by looking at how humans evolved. As you do this, you will discover just how beautiful and powerful the truth is. Best of all, you won't have to do any math or learn a new vocabulary to understand all of this.

You will see why the different mainstream and "far out" interpretations just don't matter that much. You have far less control over some parts of your life than you think. You also have far more control than you can imagine over other parts of your life. Most importantly, you are perfect just the way you are!

The perfection inside all of us often hides behind conflicting impulses. Do you ever feel like you're being pulled in two directions at the same time? The desire for success and happiness inspires you to move forward. Your negative feelings and unproductive behaviors keep holding you back. It's like driving a car with one foot on the gas and the other on the brake wondering why you're not getting anywhere.

People in this situation often feel they need to "improve" themselves by fixing whatever is wrong with them. The self-improvement effort often involves making an effort to adopt positive thoughts, feelings, and beliefs in order to "attract" what they want according to the Law of Attraction.

People who try this eventually lose their happy face as it slowly dawns on them that all the trumped-up happiness in the world isn't doing anything to change their lives—or themselves—for the better.

This book shows you how to use your power effectively by showing you that your beliefs are nothing more than opinions. Opinions may or may not be true. Either way, they are far less important than you might think in many ways.

You don't need to put on a happy face. You don't need to try to "attract" or "manifest" anything. You don't need to feel like there is some great secret out there waiting for you. Everything you need and more already exists inside you. All you need to do is make what you want real. We will show you how to do this.

The Law of Attraction tells us that anything is possible. The trick is to make what you want not only possible but probable by rigging the game for success. It's like walking into a casino and changing the rules of blackjack or any other game to increase your odds of winning. Most of us go our entire lives taking steps to make sure we don't win. You probably fall into this category because you are reading this book.

You already know how to play the game because you are already a master of setting yourself up to lose. This book explains why you do this and how you can play the same game to win.

Each of us wants the same things:

- Productive, fulfilling work
- Enough money to not have to worry about it
- Good physical, mental, emotional, and spiritual health
- Loving bonds with others
- Fun and leisure
- A long and happy life

Achieving all of these goals begins with a desire for change and at least a glimmer of hope and belief that change is possible. Freeing yourself to make those changes involves letting go by dropping old habits and taking the correct action to make what you want real. It's that simple, at least in theory.

In practice, it is very easy to think we are taking the right action when all we are doing is repeating the same old patterns. We are very good at fooling ourselves. Our brains are hard-wired to do everything it takes to remain in our current patterns and will invent any excuse to keep doing the same old things. On the plus side, this same brain wiring can ensure that you stay in your new pattern once you understand the process.

Most self-help experts agree that action is the key to success. They are correct even though they almost always say "attract" when what they really mean is "realize" as in "make real." Don't worry if none of this makes sense to you right now. We'll explain everything as we go.

Get in, sit down, and hold on tight. It's going to be a fantastic ride!

Jim Britt

Anthony Hernandez

Table of Contents

Chapter 1: Something is Wrong

We have asked thousands of people the same two very simple questions that we are about to ask you:

1. Do you believe in the Law of Attraction?
2. Is the Law of Attraction working for you by making positive changes in your life?

If you answered "no" to the second question then you are not alone. Just about everybody says "yes" to the first question. Almost every single person answers "no" to the second question with only a very few saying "yes" or that they are unsure. Even after giving these answers, these same people are all shocked when we announce that the Law of Attraction does not work. Something is wrong.

If you have been trying to use the Law of Attraction in your own life without seeing the results you want then there are a few things you need to do right now:

- Stop trying to attract and manifest your ideal life. It has not worked. It is not working. It will not ever work.
- Stop pretending that you already have everything you want and more. You don't. None of us do.
- Stop imagining that your bills are actually checks. If your bank won't accept them as deposits to your account then all the imagination in the world will not change that.
- If you are sick then seek medical attention immediately. Keeping a positive attitude can and will help you recover but don't ever rely on that alone.

- Acknowledge that you are not living your ideal life and that fantasizing about it is not getting you anywhere. If you intend to change your life then that intention is only the first step.
- Live within your means.
- Face the fact that there is no magical shortcut from where you are to where you want to go.
- Don't beat yourself up for believing in the Law of Attraction and don't blame the self-help expert who created the program you have been using. The Law of Attraction is real but has limits that very few people know about.
- Understand that you have far less control over most of your life than you think you do.
- Understand that you have far more control over parts of your life than you ever imagined possible.
- Know that you have the potential to achieve just about anything you want to achieve.
- Resolve to make your ideal life real.
- Learn why the Law of Attraction does not work… and what you can do about it.

The first step is to understand what the Law of Attraction is and where it came from. Let's get started.

Chapter 2: Explaining the Law of Attraction

It has been difficult to find a self-help system that is not based on The Law of Attraction ever since Oprah, Larry King, and Ellen popularized *The Secret* by Rhonda Byrne in 2006. *The Secret* sold hundreds of thousands of copies within hours. Millions of copies have been selling ever since. Other self-help experts have sold millions of copies of other works ever since the Law of Attraction became a household term. Small wonder that the rush to ride the coattails of these authors remains alive and well today.

Different experts explain the Law of Attraction in different ways and some of them say "Law of Attraction" when they are really talking about something completely different. This chapter looks at the Law of Attraction in its purest form. We will analyze all this in later chapters.

A Brief History

The Law of Attraction came about during the New Thought movement of the early nineteenth century. This movement believed that positive thoughts cause positive results while negative thoughts cause negative results. For example, thinking that you have all the money you need will attract more money and thinking that you need more money will attract the need for money. This is why anyone trying to use the Law of Attraction must act as if they already have their ideal life.

The term "Law of Attraction" first appeared in the 1906 book *Thought Vibration* by William Walker Atkinson. It appeared again in the 1907 title *Prosperity Through Thought Force* by Bruce MacLelland in which he claimed that "You are what you think, not what you think you are." In 1910, *The Science of Getting Rich* by Wallace D. Wattles interpreted Hindu ideas to mean that believing in and focusing on what you want will attract—or manifest—that goal, while negative thoughts will manifest negative results. Just having the belief and focus is enough to make things happen.

The 1928 book *The Law of Success in 16 Lessons* by Napoleon Hill contains many indirect references to the Law of Attraction. Hill's *Think and Grow Rich* appeared in 1937 and has sold more than sixty million copies to date. Hill explains that one must control one's thoughts and the energy behind those thoughts in order to attract other thoughts and bring about ultimate success.

Other authors ran with this concept but the Law of Attraction did not reach the masses and become a household term until *The Secret* and other programs such as the movie *What the Bleep Do We Know?* came along. If nothing else, *The Secret* has been a viral marketing triumph and a testament to the power of word-of-mouth advertising; however, just because millions of people believe something does not make it true. For example, millions of people used to believe that the world is flat and that the sun revolves around the Earth. Today we know that the world is round and that it is the Earth that goes around the sun.

What are some of the things you used to believe that you now know are not true? Take a few moments to think of a few examples and how learning the truth has affected you.

Inside The Secret

The Secret says that famous people such as, "Plato, Shakespeare, Newton, Hugo, Beethoven, Lincoln, Emerson, Edison, [and] Einstein" guard the ultimate secret to life, love, wealth, anything one could ever want. This statement seems to hint at some long-running conspiracy such as the fictional Holy Grail plot that powers *The Da Vinci Code* by Dan Brown.

Ms. Byrne describes her amazingly lucky search for the Law of Attraction and the "modern day practitioners" of this ancient art. The rest of the book consists of quotes by these practitioners. For example, Bob Proctor says, "The Secret gives you anything you want: happiness, health, and wealth." Joe Vitale says that, "You can have, do, or be anything you want." John Assaraf agrees by saying that, "We can have whatever it is that we choose. I don't care how big it is."

Do these claims match your reality? Do you consider yourself happy, healthy, and wealthy right now? Do you really have everything you want? Can you do or be anything you want? What are some of the things you want that you don't have? Why do you think you don't you have these things?

Explaining the Law of Attraction

The Secret and other Law of Attraction experts explain that the universe obeys natural laws that work together in a very delicate balance. Life as we know it would not be possible without this balance. This much is true; the universe appears to be very finely tuned to support life. Scientists refer to this as the *anthropic principle*.

The essence of the Law of Attraction is that "like attracts like." Whatever you focus on becomes a bigger part of your life. Complaining about something tells the universe to give you more things to complain about. Positive thoughts and words will attract more good things, experiences, and people into your life like a magnet. This works because the universe delivers whatever you ask of it.

These experts tell us that the Law of Attraction is the most powerful natural law in the universe. Everybody everywhere is always attracting everything good and bad into their lives. As

Bob Proctor explains it, "Whatever is going on in your mind, you are attracting to you. Every thought of yours is a real thing—a force."

This means that everybody always uses the Law of Attraction whether they know it or not. Successful people think about abundance and wealth while avoiding negative thoughts that could bring them down. People who do not have everything they want are not using the Law of Attraction properly.

The Law of Attraction works because each thought has its own frequency just like a TV station. Thoughts go out into the universe like a cosmic dinner delivery order that always arrives piping hot. One frequency orders pizza. Change the frequency and you could end up ordering Chinese. Thinking about tasting the cheesy pepperoni goodness and feeling your happy tummy is a surefire way to get pizza. Thinking about how you really don't want Chinese food is a great way to end up with a plate of fried rice and pot stickers.

Honestly, have you ever ended up in a Chinese restaurant because you really didn't want chow mein? This may seem like a very silly question but that is just what people who believe in the Law of Attraction are saying.

The whole secret of the Law of Attraction is that focusing on what you want as if you already had it guarantees results. Thinking about things you don't want brings those things into your life because the universe only hears "Chinese" or "debt" while skipping over the "I really don't want..." or "I need to get out of..." parts. The subject of the thought is what counts, not the context.

The Secret says that it is impossible to have negative thoughts while feeling good at the same time. Bad feelings are the universe warning you to cheer up fast before you start manifesting bad things. Bernard Beckwith says that, "You can begin right now to feel healthy. You can begin to feel prosperous. You can begin to feel the love that's surrounding you, even if it's not there. And what will happen is the universe will correspond to the nature of your song. The universe will correspond to the nature of that inner feeling and manifest, because that's the way you feel." Lisa Nichols agrees when she says that, "Your thoughts and your feelings create your life. It will always be that way. Guaranteed!"

This much is very true. You can choose to be happy about your life just as it is today. You can choose to make the best of whatever situation you are in. You don't need to have everything you want in order to be happy right now.

Just remember that happiness by itself will not change your circumstances, only how you see them. There is a big difference between being happy with your situation and having a completely different situation.

Placing Your Cosmic Pizza Order

Most of us know the story of Aladdin's magical lamp. Rubbing the lamp summons the genie to make his wishes come true. Aladdin need only ask for pizza to get it. Proponents of the Law of Attraction say that the same idea works for everyone. Making a wish alerts the universe to set the cosmic kitchen into motion.

Putting the Law of Attraction to work uses the following three-step process:

1. Place the order. Joe Vitale says, "It's like having the Universe as your catalogue. You flip through it and say, 'I'd like to have this experience and I'd like to have that product and I'd like to have a person like that.' It is you placing your order with the Universe. It's really that easy."

2. Believe that you already have whatever it is you want. Never mind that you may not be able to see or feel it yet. Keep your thoughts at the right frequency by using affirmations such as, "I have a gorgeous blonde girlfriend who loves me," "That

delicious pizza is in my tummy right now," "I have a million dollars in the bank," etc. Want a new car? Go test drive that car. The more you do this, the more likely you are to receive it. You will wake up one morning and it will be there, easy as that!

3. Receive your order and feel both grateful and happy. Gratitude and happiness are the keys to manifesting whatever you want from another pizza to a beach house, yacht, or Mr. Right. All you need to do is answer the door when you hear the doorbell. This little bit of action won't feel like work.

You cannot have more than you have now unless you are grateful for what you do have. All ungrateful thoughts go out into the universe and come back to you as bad feelings to alert you to the danger of further loss. Always be grateful for the things you are "attracting" as well. Make sure to think happy, grateful thoughts as you drift off to sleep each night. Always find ways to work gratitude and happiness into your life and habits.

This is great advice for life. Choosing to be happy with your current situation is a great way to reduce stress and anxiety and help you focus your mind on opportunities instead of challenges. It may be as easy as not complaining anymore. Learning to manage what you have is a great way to learn how to manage more. Start where you are. Just don't get ahead of yourself.

The local pizza parlor may promise delivery within 30 minutes but the universe has no such guarantees because time itself is an illusion. *The Secret* says that, "Quantum physicists and Einstein tell us is that everything is happening simultaneously." and "Any time delay you experience is due to your delay in getting to the place of believing, knowing, and feeling that you already have it."

In other words, the reason you are not getting what you want is because you don't believe you have it already. You don't have money because you don't believe you have it. You don't have a loving relationship because you don't believe you have one. If you have tried to use the Law of Attraction to no avail then you know that this walks a fine line between making the best of your situation and delusion.

What Can the Law of Attraction Do for You?

The Secret explains that the Law of Attraction can do anything you want because the universe does not take no for an answer. Want to lose weight? Visualize yourself at your ideal weight. Buy smaller clothes. Don't think about the weight you need to lose unless you want it to stick with you. After all, "Food cannot cause you to put on weight, unless you think it can," and "A person cannot think 'thin thoughts' and be fat. It completely defies the Law of Attraction." Pizza and ice cream for everyone!

Expect checks in your mailbox instead of bills. See your bills as checks for ten times the amount due. Don't think about the debt you are in. Keep expecting that check and it will come to you. You can afford anything you want no matter how little money you have right now. Be happy. Happier people are richer people. Don't worry about other people. There is more than enough to go around.

Want a new relationship or to fix up an existing one? Be happy! Focus on having that relationship with that lusty busty blonde and concentrate on her good qualities. Love yourself if you want to attract people who will love you.

Feeling a bit under the weather? Got cancer or any other disease or condition? Don't blame bacteria and viruses. Stress is your real problem. Disease is a feedback loop for stress that you can break out of with love, gratitude, and seeing yourself perfectly healthy. *The Secret* includes a testimonial from a woman who claims to have used the Law of Attraction to cure her breast cancer. Bob Proctor says that, "Disease cannot live in a body that's in a healthy emotional state."

The Secret even says that one can use the Law of Attraction to "put a stopper in death," as author J.K. Rowling put it in *Harry Potter and the Sorcerer's Stone*. John Assaraf says that, "Beliefs about aging are all in our minds. Release those thoughts and focus on eternal youth."

Hmm...

Is It Real?

Is the Law of Attraction real? Yes. Is the Law of Attraction as powerful as its many adherents claim? Yes, but only under very limited circumstances. This is the missing ingredient.

Is the Law of Attraction based on solid science? Sort of. It is based on "far out" interpretations of quantum physics. Quantum physics is the most accurate and powerful science ever devised by humankind. The fact that the Law of Attraction is based on "far out" science does not make it wrong. It does mean that we need to take a hard look at the science itself to see what conclusions we can make.

Is there more to this story? Absolutely. We need to look at the science to figure out the missing ingredient and why this makes the Law of Attraction all but useless for daily life. We need to learn a thing or two about physics in order to understand both how the Law of Attraction works and why it is so limited. Don't worry, there won't be much math!

Chapter 3: The Science

Gasps of shock ripple across the room every time we announce that the Law of Attraction does not work. Then the questions begin. Many of these questions revolve around quantum physics and the many claims self-help experts make about what science can and cannot prove. These are good questions that deserve answers.

Answering those questions requires a brief explanation of the science that makes the Law of Attraction both real and useless for improving your life. This explanation will also point the way toward the missing ingredient that makes all the difference in the world. Having this knowledge will help you understand why the Law of Attraction does not work and how you can take real steps toward getting the life you want. Please keep that in mind as you read the next few pages.

Classical Physics

The word physics comes from the Greek word *physis,* which means, "the true nature of things." Sir Isaac Newton founded modern physics over four hundred years ago. Most people who talk about physics are talking about Newtonian or *classical* physics. Quantum physics and later theories do not prove Newton wrong. On the contrary, Newton's discoveries and equations are still in use today.

Classical physics has no room for the Law of Attraction. It treats the universe as a giant machine where one can know both past and future based on what is happening at any given moment. This "clockwork" universe runs on cause and effect and consists of a single absolute reality without any cosmic intelligence or soul.

The entire universe seemed on the verge of complete explanation by the end of the nineteenth century. Some people thought that the end of science was near and that nothing new remained to discover. In the year 1900, Lord Kelvin famously said that only "two small clouds" remained on the horizon. The first cloud was how light travels. The second cloud was how objects radiate energy when light hits them.

Lord Kelvin could not have been more wrong. His "small clouds" opened the door to quantum physics, relativity, and the Law of Attraction. Quantum physics is the most accurate science ever discovered. It is also the most extensively tested and validated science in human history. It may therefore surprise you to learn that it can only give us the probability that something will happen. For example, quantum physics can tell us the chances of finding a particle in a given location at a given time but not much more.

Quantum physics opened the door for the Law of Attraction by doing away with the idea of a predictable clockwork universe.

Into the Quantum

The quantum world behaves in some very strange ways that make the Law of Attraction both possible and real. For example:

- Reality is grainy. There are such things as a shortest possible time and a smallest possible mass.
- We can never know everything there is to know. The more we know about some things, the less we can know about others.
- Matter can turn into energy and vice-versa.
- Particles can vanish from one location and reappear in another location.

- The total amount of energy in the universe is zero.
- Solid matter is not solid. It can behave as either solid particles or as waves of energy.
- Just about anything you can imagine is possible.

These are just a few of the strange things happening at the deepest foundations of reality. We live in a truly amazing universe.

Entanglement

Grab two objects. Do anything you want to them and then send them on their way. Common sense says that neither object will "remember" the encounter or behave any differently. Quantum objects such as atoms and particles are different. They do remember encountering the other quantum object. They also know what their partner is doing and do the exact same thing at the exact same time no matter how far away they are from each other. Scientists call this partnership *entanglement.* They refer to the instant interactions between entangled objects as *nonlocality.* For example, bouncing one photon off a mirror causes its entangled partner to behave as though it also hit a mirror even when there is no mirror in its path.

Every particle in the universe was entangled during the Big Bang. The separation we see between objects is an illusion, including time itself. The entire universe and everything in it is connected in ways we are only beginning to understand. All objects in the universe from the smallest particle to the largest galaxy exist at all times and in all places at once. This is called *superposition.*

Measurement "collapses" the superposition into a single position at a single time. Focus your attention on a nearby object and then look away from it. The object could be anywhere in the universe at any point in time as long as you are not looking at it.

Turning back to look at it "collapses" the object into place, which is usually the last place you looked at it.

Nonlocality means that particles can jump from any spot in the universe to any other spot in an instant. This literally means that just about anything you can imagine is possible. As one writer said, "Prepare your oven and then sit back and wait; there is a nonzero probability that a turkey from a nearby grocery store will materialize in your oven."

Entanglement and nonlocality tell us that our universe is a mesh of forces, fields, and matter that can come and go at will. Many self-help experts see this as proof that everything in the universe is connected to everything else and that the Law of Attraction is real. They are technically correct. The problems begin when we try to use this to attract and manifest things in our own lives.

Waves of Possibility

Picture the universe as a table covered by a wrinkled tablecloth. The flat surface of the table represents all of the points of space and time within the universe. The wrinkled surface of the tablecloth represents the possibility of finding a particle at any place and time. Flat areas represent low chances. Peaks represent the highest chances. The height of any point on the tablecloth above the table represents the chances of finding whatever you are looking for at that exact point in time and space. The tablecloth may have one, two, a few, or many wrinkles and high spots.

The shape of the tablecloth itself represents a *quantum waveform* or simply *waveform* for short. All waveforms extend across the entire universe and never shrink all the way to zero. This plus nonlocality are what make the Law of Attraction real.

Here is a real-world example of a waveform in action: Anthony's son Logan goes to school on weekdays. His waveform instantly spreads across the entire universe the moment he walks out the front door. Logan's waveform is extremely high right over his desk during the school day. This means that Logan has an excellent chance of being where he is supposed to be during school hours but he could also be anywhere in the universe at any point in time.

Logan carries a cell phone with a built-in GPS tracker that lets Anthony monitor his location. Running the tracker program measures Logan's position. That indirect measurement "collapses" the waveform. For example, the tracker may say that Logan is within forty yards of his desk. Using the tracker and observing the result thus "collapses" the waveform to a circle that is eighty yards across. At that moment, Logan is guaranteed to be somewhere within that circle.

Walking into Logan's classroom and seeing him there is a direct measurement that collapses his waveform to an exact location. There is no chance that Logan is anywhere else when that measurement happens. His waveform then spreads back across the entire universe the minute Anthony looks away.

The waveform determines how the superposition we mentioned a few moments ago will become an actual position in space and time. Every object in the universe only exists as a superposition governed by a waveform unless and until something "collapses" the waveform into a single actuality by taking a measurement.

The Secret is right to say that everything in the universe exists in all places and at all times at once. For example, Logan exists everywhere and everywhen in the universe at once until looking at him or using his cell phone tracker collapses his waveform to a certain place at a certain time.

Accepting the waveform means accepting that possibility is just as real as actuality. Possibility may in fact be more real than actuality because possibility is timeless while actuality only exists for an instant.

There is a chance that just about anything you can imagine will come true. That turkey could indeed pop right into your oven.

You could suddenly find all the money you ever wanted in your refrigerator, attract your ideal relationship, etc. The waveform makes this possible and proves that the Law of Attraction is very real.

The waveform also tells us why the Law of Attraction does not work and why you should immediately stop trying to attract or manifest anything in your life. Just because something is possible does not make it likely to happen any time soon. For example, what are the odds that you could manifest a million dollars?

Don't worry about the actual numbers just yet. For now, let's make the math very simple by pretending that a one hundred-dollar bill is made of one hundred atoms and that each atom has a fifty-fifty chance of being where you want it when you want it. Having fifty-fifty odds means that you have a fifty percent chance of manifesting a single atom and that you can expect one atom to show up for every two attempts.

These odds shrink by half for every additional atom you try to manifest. The odds of getting two atoms to cooperate are once for every four attempts. The odds of getting three atoms to cooperate are once for every eight attempts. Four atoms cooperate once in every sixteen attempts, five atoms once in thirty two attempts, six atoms once in sixty four attempts, and so on.

Your odds of manifesting all one hundred atoms on command are extremely low. How low? The universe is roughly fourteen billion years old. You would have to wait many thousands of times longer than that for all one hundred atoms to show up. Put it this way: If the entire age of the universe were one day then you would have to wait billions of years to manifest a single hundred-dollar bill. Appendix B gives you the math in detail.

This is bad news for your finances. The worse news is that you need ten thousand of these hundred-dollar bills to make one million dollars. The ugly news is that a real dollar bill contains not one hundred but many trillions of atoms. The worst news is that the odds of a single atom manifesting on command are far less than fifty-fifty.

Self-help experts are right to say that quantum physics proves the Law of Attraction is real. What they don't know is that quantum physics also proves that the Law of Attraction is useless. This is why all your attempts to attract and manifest your ideal life will never work and why you should stop trying right now.

If something sounds too good to be true then it probably is. The Law of Attraction sounds wonderful. It does not get much more positive than, "If you can dream it, you can do it." It is no wonder that programs built on the Law of Attraction are so popular.

These programs are correct on a technical level. Unfortunately, they are utterly wrong on a practical level because very few people understand that the waveform cuts both ways by making everything possible while at the same time making only a few of those possibilities likely to actually happen.

We don't for a moment believe that the creators of programs based on the Law of Attraction set out to deceive anybody. We simply believe that the concept of the Law of Attraction is based on understanding only the theoretical workings of quantum mechanics without considering the practical implications of trying to put that theoretical knowledge to use.

Exceptions Prove the Rule

You may have a hard time believing us because every self-help expert tells inspiring stories about people who successfully used the Law of Attraction to achieve their goals. These stories are almost certainly not true because they most probably have alternative explanations that do not involve the Law of Attraction. We are not suggesting that anyone is lying! People genuinely believe that the Law of Attraction caused their success but the math does not support that belief.

Let's give these people the benefit of the doubt for a moment by forgetting the math and assuming that some of the stories are true. Do these true stories prove us wrong when we say that the Law of Attraction does not work? No!

Consider this: About eight million people visit a famous cave in Lourdes, France every year because they believe that the water flowing from the spring inside has healing powers. Sixty-six of these people experienced "miraculous" cures. The people who visit Lourdes obviously know about these cures just like you know of people who may have succeeded because of the Law of Attraction.

The stories about Lourdes fail to mention that sick people all over the world sometimes experience spontaneous healing. In fact, the general population of people with terminal illnesses experience these cures at a rate that is many times higher than the cure rate for people who visit Lourdes. Thus, there is no miracle cure in that cave. There is nothing special in the water.

The people who travel to Lourdes are far less likely to be cured than those who don't. The water did not cure those people and the Law of Attraction is most probably not responsible for the success stories you hear from self-help experts.

Stories about miracle cures and the Law of Attraction fascinate and inspire us precisely because they describe very rare events. Think about the nightly news. The stories you see are all rare events. We hear about every plane crash because very few planes crash. You don't hear about the many thousands of flights that land safely every day.

People get scared of the things they see and hear in the news because bad things do happen to good people every day. The dramatic images and news reporting make it easy to forget that an average person has a far better chance of being struck by lightning from a clear blue sky than they do of experiencing the tragedies described in the news. The day you witness a plane crash and do not hear about it on the news is the day you should stop flying because that will be the day that plane crashes are so common that they are no longer news!

People can and do lift themselves from rags to riches and achieve their ideal lives. Some of them may do it using the Law of Attraction but that is never the way to bet. The safe bet that those people who take action to make changes regardless of their beliefs and emotions succeed at a far higher rate than those who sit around trying to attract and manifest paradise out of thin air. Some people who take action may believe that the Law of Attraction caused their success but that is absolutely not the case.

If you are one of the many people trying to use the Law of Attraction to improve your life then we again urge you to stop unless you have many trillions of years to spend waiting.

We also urge you to resist any temptation you may feel to feel guilty, duped, or in any way negative about buying into the Law of Attraction. The time and energy you invested there was well spent. What you are learning now is not about correcting any past mistake. It is about taking the next step in your personal growth just like you have been doing your whole life. Above all, don't beat yourself up or feel discouraged. You are on the cusp of learning how to put the knowledge you have gained to work!

To Learn More

This is all the science you need to understand why the Law of Attraction does not work as advertised but there is far more to learn. Appendix B provides additional information about time, how scientists interpret quantum physics, and the possibility of the Universal Mind that many Law of Attraction programs talk about. We also invite you to pick up a copy of *Through the Looking Glass: The Science Behind the Law of Realization* for an even more detailed look. Meanwhile, let's use what we learned to take another look at the Law of Attraction.

* * *

Chapter 4: Revisiting the Law of Attraction

The article *Science behind 'The Secret?'* released by ABC News says that, "Critics say *The Secret* is not only wrong, it is dangerous, leading people to believe you can get what you want, whether it's getting rich, curing disease, or losing weight simply by thinking positively about it." This article includes the following quotes:

- "I want to be very clear that there is no evidence that people attract cancer by their thoughts." and, "If some person chose to strictly follow the steps in this book, there is a risk that they could die needlessly." - Dr. Richard Wender, president of the American Cancer Society.
- "If by 'Law of Attraction,' they have this notion of having a thought and it attracts like thoughts, I can assure you that quantum physics has nothing to say about that." - Brian Greene, physicist.
- "Look, I've never met any of those guys, but I have zero evidence that any of them would've held on to any fundamental secret about the world and not shared it." - Brian Greene, physicist.

These quotes refer to *The Secret* but they apply equally well to just about any program based on the Law of Attraction. Any one of these criticisms is strong enough to sink the Law of Attraction on its own and the combined effect is devastating. That plus the science we explained in the last chapter should be enough to convince you that the Law of Attraction is absolutely useless as a tool for changing your life. It is little more than wishful thinking that does not and cannot work.

Creating Our Reality

It is true that objective reality does not exist. Each of us creates our own personal reality using this process:

1. Our earliest experiences (that probably begin before birth) create our feelings and emotions
2. Our feelings and emotions create our thoughts.
3. The more we think in a certain way, the more we come to believe it.
4. Beliefs and emotions drive us to act in certain ways.
5. Our actions create results that validate our original beliefs.
6. Lather, rinse, repeat.

Humans are emotional creatures on our deepest levels. Our logic spends most of its time rationalizing and validating our beliefs and emotions.

Each emotion we experience creates a chemical cocktail that courses through our veins and attaches to cells all over our bodies. These emotional chemicals connect to the same places used by addictive drugs like heroin.

This means that we are all literally addicted to our emotions. Each of us is a junkie who is addicted to certain emotional patterns. We keep repeating the same old cycles and living the same old pattern in order to keep feeding that addiction.

This cycle of addiction exists because nature did not place humans at the top of the food chain. A naked human in the wild is at far more risk of being killed and eaten by a wild animal than the animals are of being killed and eaten by that human. We are prey animals whether we like it or not.

All prey animals need to know how to survive by avoiding predators. They do this by learning a set of behaviors that will keep them alive. All newborn animals interpret all of the information they receive as survival instructions. These instructions and the emotions that go with them form core beliefs and start the cycle of addiction.

Humans are no different. Infants have no idea what civilization is or how it works. All they know is that they must absorb and follow what they learn in order to avoid being killed and eaten.

The Secret says that emotions alert us to bad thoughts and warn us that we are about to manifest bad things. This is wrong because it assumes that logic drives humans and not emotions. Conscious thought can make us take actions beyond our addictive patterns. This puts us into a state of withdrawal that is just like withdrawing from drugs like heroin. We can start to change our lives but soon find ourselves back in the same old rut.

The real secret is to take action to make your dreams real and to keep going no matter what. Reward yourself for every little step instead of punishing yourself for not being where you want to be. The whole idea is to replace your current emotional addictions with new ones. You do this by letting go of the negative to give yourself more room for the positive. We will start discussing letting go in Chapter 13.

We are emotional prey animals who can never escape the fear of being killed and eaten and who will always follow our survival instincts to the letter. We cannot change that. What we can do is reprogram those instincts.

Inherent Contradictions

Proponents of the Law of Attraction say that we can do, have, and be absolutely anything we want if we follow the three steps we discussed in Chapter 2:

1. Place our order for what we want.
2. Visualize having that order fulfilled
3. Be happy and grateful at all cost.

On one hand, this must work because the Universal Mind is all-powerful and unable to refuse us our every wish. On the other hand, Bernard Beckwith says in *The Secret* that, "We live in a universe in which there are laws just as there is a law of gravity. If you fall off a building it doesn't matter if you're a good person or a bad person, you're going to hit the ground."

On one hand, the Law of Attraction says we can have everything and anything we want up to and including defying age and death. On the other hand, it seems that flying is not on the list of possibilities. The universe seems both capable and incapable of giving us everything we want. The Universal Mind seems both powerful and helpless.

Which is it?

It turns out that Mr. Beckwith is correct: The universe must obey its own laws because making one exception risks making another and another until the very fabric of space-time that makes life possible falls apart.

Assume for the moment that any program claiming that some "Universal Mind," "God," "higher power," etc. created the universe is absolutely correct on this point. It is self-evident that a Universal Mind capable of creating a universe as orderly as ours must be rational to its core. A universe cannot support life without being self-consistent. A self-consistent universe cannot possibly break its own laws.

This is why the quantum waveform means that you cannot have your cake and eat it too except under very limited circumstances. All things are possible but some things are much more likely than other things. The universe has a little wiggle room but not much.

Quantum physics can only give us probabilities and we can never know all there is to know. The universe has some randomness built right into it. We cannot avoid this randomness. This is yet another reason why we cannot simply manifest anything we want and why the Law of Attraction is not the tool to use for self-improvement.

What does this mean for you? Never jump off any tall buildings. Seek medical help if you get sick. If you are overweight then eat less and exercise more. If you want more money then take steps to make more money. If you want a new relationship then go out and look for one. If you want to fix an existing relationship then take steps to fix it. The bottom line is that you need to use the laws of human nature and physics to your advantage.

The Universe Is Not Stupid

Stay with the assumption that the universe ultimately consists of a Universal Mind that is the source of everything. More than one Law of Attraction program claims that this Universal Mind created the universe and everything in it. They then go on to claim that this same Universal Mind cannot understand basic grade-school grammar. This is why you must focus on what you do want such as money and never on your debt.

Ask yourself whether this claim makes any sense. Can the Universal Mind possibly be that powerful and yet that stupid? Have you ever ended up in an Italian restaurant because you absolutely did not want pasta? We submit that any Universal Mind that is unable to comprehend the grammar it created would be incapable of creating the universe to begin with.

Shared Reality

People who claim we can manifest anything we want using the Law of Attraction forget that we share many aspects of our individual realities. Imagine that you and another person are approaching an intersection with a traffic light that can be either red or green. Both of you want the light to be green and try to manifest that reality. The light cannot be both red and green at the same time. Whose choice counts?

This waveform has two possible outcomes that are equally possible. This means that you and the other person each get the green light half the time. This simple example proves that nobody can get whatever they want all the time. We cannot not have an orderly universe without waveforms and none of us could be alive in a chaotic universe. The universe cannot and will not contradict itself no matter how hard the pieces known as "you," "Anthony," "Jim," and others try.

Different people may have different levels of willpower. Stronger willpower may be able to beat the odds. If this is true then someone with perfect willpower could possibly have everything she wants whenever she wants it. We can never know because there is no such thing as a person with perfect will power. Each of us is capable of making dramatic changes in our lives in a very short period of time but this is nowhere near the same as manifesting your every wish.

The 1999 movie *Mystery Men* includes a character named Invisible Boy who is only invisible when nobody is looking. You may be convinced that you can do something. For example, you may believe in your heart that you can fly. This may be your reality. The problem is that you must share that reality with other people. If you think you can fly and your friend thinks you can't then you can't.

The shared reality is the lowest common denominator and just about everyone believes that people cannot fly. This means that people cannot fly no matter how much they may think they can. It's that simple. Anything else would be chaos. Anything else and none of us would be here to discuss this.

Disentanglement

Entangled particles march in perfect step with their partners because of nonlocality. Everything in the universe is entangled with everything else. Entanglement never shrinks to zero. We are all one as *The Secret* says. What *The Secret* does not say is that entanglement can exist on many different levels.

Photons created under carefully controlled conditions can be very entangled. Bouncing one entangled photon off a mirror causes its partner to bounce as if it had hit its own mirror. People who are intimately involved with each other cannot reliably make their partners do anything but can influence thoughts and feelings. This is an example of a weaker level of entanglement because nobody can force another person to think or do anything.

Any entanglement that may exist between you and a luxury yacht in the pages of *Robb Report* magazine is weak enough for us to ignore. The Law of Attraction again fails to live up to expectations.

The Quantum Tsunami

Matter can turn into energy. Energy can turn into matter. All things exist in a superposition that covers all possibilities at once. The waveform contains all of the possibilities and extends across the entire universe. The fact that the waveform never shrinks to zero between measurements means that you can manifest anything you want. You could at any moment find yourself orbiting Pluto or discover a million-dollar check in your mailbox.

Don't hold your breath waiting for either event to happen. The Law of Attraction is correct but the odds of manifesting anything are very low. You could literally expect to wait trillions of years before manifesting something becomes statistically probable.

The fact that the odds of atoms simply wandering off by themselves or not obeying the many natural laws are very low also means that you can be virtually certain that the pen you put in your desk drawer is still there even though you cannot see it right now. Your pen is in a superposition because of the waveform but the waveform is extremely high in your desk drawer and extremely low everywhere else.

Remember that the seeming exceptions only prove the rule. We saw in Chapter 3 that the people who visited Lourdes healed at a far lower rate than the general population. The supposed miracle is nothing but simple statistics.

The quantum waveform makes the Law of Attraction real. It is also a tsunami that destroys any ability to use the Law of Attraction for any practical purpose.

Debunking the Law of Attraction

The Law of Attraction ends up being nothing more than a convenient theoretical shorthand for everything we know from quantum physics and other sciences with zero practical value. So what should we make of the self-help experts who sell the Law of Attraction as a tool?

Critics and mainstream science scoff at the self-help industry. This is unfortunate because the self-help industry has the power to change many lives. The problem is that scientific misunderstanding and misinformation taints the good material and makes everything suspect. On the other hand, most self-help experts need only make minor updates to their material to conform to mainstream science.

These experts may not know much about quantum physics but they do know how to make positive life changes. Many of them are living examples of lives that have turned around. They come from a place of wanting to help people. Their material is very helpful even if the parts about the Law of Attraction are a bit off. If anything you have seen from any expert has helped you then nothing we are saying here will change that.

Chapter 5: The Real Secret

Jim recently received a call from his friend Helen.

"I'm going crazy," Helen said. "I'm using the Law of Attraction just like I'm supposed to but it's not working. What's wrong with me?"

Jim laughed. "Nothing's wrong with you, Helen. You've just discovered something very important about the Law of Attraction. It doesn't work."

"It doesn't?" Helen was shocked. "Why not?"

"You do a lot of driving, "Jim said. "When you get hungry for a hamburger, do you try to manifest one right there in your car or do you get off the highway and go find a restaurant?"

It was Helen's turn to laugh. "I go to a restaurant of course. Trying to manifest a hamburger in my car would be silly!"

"Then why are you trying to manifest more money in your life?" Jim asked.

There was a long pause before Helen finally asked, "Is there science behind this?"

"Yes," Jim replied. "The same science that proves the Law of Attraction real also proves why it doesn't work. Say you're trying to manifest a million dollars. To manifest a single hundred-dollar bill..."

Jim gave Helen the example we saw in Chapter 3 about trying to manifest money.

"Wow," Helen said when Jim had finished. "That is so refreshing. I am so relieved to know I'm not the problem. And if it takes that long to manifest a hamburger, imagine how much longer it would take to manifest a cheeseburger with all those extra atoms!"

Helen learned a very simple yet powerful lesson that day: If you want something then you need to go out and get what you want. Trying to make what you want come to you won't work. This is the difference between attraction and realization. Attraction is little more than wishful thinking. Realization is taking action to make real your desired outcome. Taking action toward what you want is the single best way to increase your chances of realizing your dreams.

The Law of Realization

Anything that you cannot directly or indirectly perceive could be anywhere in the universe at any point in time. Looking at that thing measures its waveform. This measurement collapses the infinite possibility into a single actuality like popping a balloon. Collapse happens according to the laws of physics and shared reality. Some possible outcomes are far more possible than others. The most common outcomes will occur far more often than the rare outcomes.

Let's return to the example of the pen in your desk drawer. Your pen is in a superposition when you cannot see it, which means that it could be anywhere in the universe at any point in time. Opening your desk drawer and looking at your pen is a measurement that instantly collapses the waveform to a single point in space and time.

You are not getting the things you want in your life either because what you want has a very low possibility of coming true or because you are not seeing an obvious solution. If you are unemployed and in debt up to your ears then chances are excellent that your mailbox will contain far more bills than checks. All the wishing and gratitude and imagining that your bills are checks will not change your situation one bit. Don't waste your time.

Whatever you are doing is causing your waveform to collapse in ways that keep your bad cycle happening. Your beliefs, emotions, thoughts, and actions are making all this happen. They are one hundred percent successful at keeping you stuck in your pattern. You are not a failure at all. You are in fact a total success.

For example, say you really want a loving relationship but refuse to go out and meet people for whatever reason. Your refusal to make yourself available makes the odds of finding that loving relationship extremely low. You are taking action to keep yourself off the market and away from prospective mates and are experiencing total success at remaining single.

Collapsing a waveform makes the possible actual. This is a natural law. We can use the term *realization* to describe the act of making something actual. We can then apply this term to the law of waveform collapse to call it the Law of Realization. The Law of Realization is the real secret to getting what you want in life.

Leaving your house to go out and meet people boosts the odds of you having that loving relationship. You don't have to know who your new love is. Just taking that action toward the goal boosts your odds of achieving that goal.

We can use the example of the table and wrinkled tablecloth to explain the difference between the Law of Attraction and the Law of Realization. Imagine Helen driving her car on the freeway and a hamburger in a roadside restaurant. Helen's waveform is very high over her location and the hamburger's waveform is very high right over the restaurant. These peaks are very far away from each other.

The Law of Attraction says that Helen can make the hamburger come to her by wanting the hamburger, imagining the yummy taste and full tummy, and being happy and grateful for the all-beef patty and sesame bun in advance. Helen realized how silly it was to think that she could make the hamburger come to her. We think you would agree that the chances of this happening are pretty low.

The Law of Realization says that Helen must move toward the hamburger. Doing this brings the peaks of the waveforms closer and closer until they merge into one when Helen reaches the restaurant and receives her order. It does not matter what Helen believes, how she feels, whether or not she wants the hamburger, or if she likes beef at all. All that matters is that she moved in a direction that made finding the hamburger more and more likely.

The Law of Attraction says that Helen had better not think about how much she really does not want a taco lest she end up at a taco stand. The Law of Realization says that not wanting a taco is a great way to predict that Helen will drive past the taco stand on her way to the hamburger joint.

Each of us is like Helen looking for a hamburger. The only way we will get that hamburger is to move toward it. This bends the waveform in a way that makes finding the hamburger more and more likely. If we keep going in the right direction then we will eventually find the hamburger. We cannot say for sure that we will find a hamburger until we see it right in front of us. We can say that going to a hamburger restaurant is a really good way to increase our odds of satisfying our craving for a hamburger.

This is the Law of Realization. This is the real secret of success.

Let's use a different food example: Imagine that everything in life is a piece of cheese. Each of us is always moving toward some of this cheese. The problem is that the cheese we are finding is often not the kind of cheese we want. We may not like the cheese we are finding and could even hate it but that is the only kind of cheese we know how to find.

We are so good at finding this bad cheese that trying to find something different makes us crave the same old stinky limburger even more. This happens because of emotional addictions that are designed to keep us from getting killed and eaten. We will look at this more in Chapter 7.

The trick is to learn what kind of cheese we like and then start finding it. We need to reprogram ourselves to be addicted to the new cheese. The fact that we have been so successful at finding the old cheese gives us strong reason to believe that we will be just as successful at finding the new cheese.

You are already using the Law of Realization all the time and it is working perfectly. All you need to do is learn how to make the Law of Realization work for you instead of against you. Your pizza, perfect mate, Swiss bank account, yacht, etc. are out there but you need to get there first before you can have them. Veruca Salt from *Willy Wonka & the Chocolate Factory* is absolutely correct to want everything NOW but that does not mean she will get her way every time or even some of the time.

* * *

Chapter 6: What Everyone Wants in Life

Each of us is a unique being with equally unique goals and dreams. We all tend to follow some very common patterns because everyone alive today wants pretty much the same things. Most of us have some of these things and some are missing from most of our lives. The following list appears in alphabetical order for convenience because everyone prioritizes this list differently.

Freedom

We all seek to be free. With freedom comes responsibility. Each person has her or his own definition of freedom and each of us must take total responsibility for obtaining and maintaining that freedom.

Your life plans and means for achieving them will crystallize as you learn who you truly are, the power you possess, and how life really works. You will refine and clarify your definition of exactly what freedom means to you as you learn these things.

Fun

We all seek to have at least some fun in our lives. Truly happy people look for the fun in everything they do. They don't chase fun and never segregate their lives into "drudgery" and "fun." Every waking moment of every day is fun for someone who is living the life he or she was meant to live.

Happiness

We all seek to be happy. Happiness is the most sought after and misunderstood commodity in the world. Everyone from the fictional princess trying to find her chance for real love to the real celebrity on drugs trying to escape their personal pain is looking for happiness.

What most people fail to realize is that happiness comes from you not at you. Happiness is a state of living fully in the moment and accepting everything that comes your way, good or not so good, as a stepping stone to learning and growing.

Health

We all seek to be able to count on our bodies to respond when asked and to be free from pain. Anyone who suffers from health problems knows that health good enough to take for granted is something we all desire.

Obtaining and maintaining this sought-after health can be challenging because we face many stresses each day. We believe that many of our real and imagined ills may stem from not accepting or following our individual paths and from projecting the past and future into the present.

Longevity

We all seek to postpone death as long as possible under normal circumstances. The best reason to delay death is to have enough time to gain the wisdom to truly appreciate all of your accomplishments. Your path to longevity becomes easier and more fulfilling when you have satisfying work that fulfills whatever mission you set for yourself in this lifetime.

Love

We all seek to build and maintain loving supportive bonds with others. The need to be wanted, cared for, and loved is the greatest of all human needs. Unfortunately, we often seek this love because of some sense of emptiness or longing to satisfy some unfilled need. This leads to codependency, divorce, infidelity, and many other problems when we realize that someone we love cannot satisfy those needs.

Love should never be the symptom of other's needs or a source of pleasure. Pleasure is temporary but love is a state of being. It's who you are. Love comes from you not at you from an outside experience. This very subtle difference is not always easy to discern yet the results are tremendous.

It is truly wonderful to seek love from a place where love itself is the need. Best of all is love that exists for its own sake without any desire or attachment.

Money

We all seek to have enough money to never have to worry about it. Money itself is nothing more than a tool for facilitating exchanges. There is nothing good or evil about money or any other tool you may have. You can use a hammer to build a home or to destroy lives. You can use a pen to spread messages of love or hate. The tool itself is not the issue. Our perceptions and emotions surrounding the tool are what matter.

Too many self-help programs equate wealth with a huge bank account and the luxuries that come with it. We define wealth as the freedom to fulfill one's life mission. If you were born to live a life of financial poverty in a spiritual outpost and you do that then you are rich. If you were born to live a life of extraordinary material abundance and you do that then you are rich. If you were born to live in a monastery but are living a lavish lifestyle then you are truly poor.

Work

We all seek to be productive in our own way and want our efforts to be a source of joy and fulfillment. We want to know that we are creating something positive and leaving a lasting legacy. The problem comes when we start defining work as the effort itself and losing focus on the desired results. This leads to struggle. Struggle causes stress. Stress causes many physical ailments up to and including premature death.

Embracing the idea that work is measured not in effort (struggle) but in output (results) can free us from much of our daily stress. Combine this with finding and living your life mission and you will be well on the path to the success you want and deserve.

Chapter 7: Humble Origins

We need to look at our evolutionary roots to understand how and why we do the things we do. Knowing where we came from helps us see where we are going and gives us hints about how our brains work. Knowing how our brains work is important because everything we think, feel, believe, and remember depends on our brain's capabilities and limitations.

Our entire lives and personal realities depend on what our brains can and cannot do. This is why knowing how our brains work is so important for achieving success in life. Animals are either predators or prey by nature. Many kinds of animals fill both roles, such as a snake that eats mice and in turn gets eaten by birds. Any animal that faces the risk of being killed and eaten exhibits at least some prey behavior.

It is tempting to think that humans are at the top of the food chain. Our technology and weapons give us powerful advantages over all other species and no other animal can match our wealth of inventions and innovation. But what happens when we leave all of our fancy toys behind? The truth about human nature is a little shocking and more than a little humbling.

One Common Ancestor

Tracing the paths of human and monkey evolution back through time leads to a common ancestor species. Evolution caused this animal to split into two separate lines that became humans and monkeys. We know this because comparing man and monkey reveals far more similarities than differences.

You may not believe in evolution. We won't argue with you. We will simply point out that human and chimpanzee DNA is very similar no matter how it got to be that way and that the comparison remains valid.

Humans share about 98% of our DNA with chimpanzees and not much less with other ape and monkey species. This is why looking at apes and monkeys is a great way to gain insight into human behavior. Let's look at our primate cousins.

A monkey is a monkey is a monkey. Some live in trees while others live on grasslands. Many different species span varying climates. Nature perfectly adapted each species to thrive in its own unique habitat. Humans evolved from the common ancestor, spread over the globe, and like our ancestors we adapted to our own local habitats.

The key difference between humans and primates may boil down to a single defective gene. This bad gene caused human jaws to weaken. This has two effects. First, an animal with a weak jaw cannot bite as hard and loses one way to defend against predators. Second, a gentler bite puts less stress on the skull. Less stress on the skull allows the brain to expand.

Think about this for a moment. If this theory is correct then human evolution began because of a genetic disorder. We may be diseased monkeys. Wow! Our origins cannot get more humble than this.

This theory also allows us to use the many similarities between humans and primates to gain some interesting insights into our own behavior. Learning how our deepest instincts work can help us learn to use them to make positive changes in our lives.

Swapping Brawn for Brains

The average monkey is far stronger that the average human on a pound-for-pound basis. The exact opposite is true about mental ability. Humans traded the ability to survive on brawn for the ability to survive by our wits. The same instincts that kept humankind alive can prevent us from having the lives we want. The good news is that we can use those instincts to our advantage if we understand how.

Built-in Limits

Let's use the example of a computer to help us look inside our own heads. Please understand that we are not saying that people are nothing but computers. All we are saying is that the computer example is a good way to explain how our brains work.

Computer hardware is the actual machinery. Software is nothing but information that the hardware stores and processes. The software cannot run without the hardware. A hardware malfunction can prevent the software from running well or at all. Software also depends on hardware for its capabilities. For example, if you have a music program but no speakers then you will not hear any music no matter how you adjust the program.

A human brain is a little like computer hardware in that it contains and executes software programs that form your thoughts, feelings, beliefs, behaviors, and memories.

Humans as Prey

Humans and monkeys evolved from the same common ancestor species. Monkeys and apes are prey animals. A naked human stands little chance against a predator animal. This is why we say that humans are prey animals far more than we are predators. We do hunt and eat meat but that does not mean that we are at the top of the food chain. Humans have been on nature's menu for millions of years. We are still on the menu.

A naked human can catch, overpower, and kill relatively few animals. Many kinds of animals can catch, overpower, and kill a naked human. We like to think that we are the masters of all we survey but the fact is that we have far more prey in us than predator. This fact holds true whether or not you believe in evolution.

Many Neanderthals ended up inside saber-toothed tigers only a few thousand years ago. Wild animals still hunt and kill humans every year. Even our own house pets sometimes kill us. Our monkey cousins who are almost but not quite human face the threat of predators at every moment of every day. That is our heritage whether we like it or not.

Most people alive today need not worry about being killed and eaten but the safety offered by modern civilization has only been around for a few thousand years. Humans and our ancestors have been hunted for millions of years. Our brains have not had time to rewire themselves to reflect modern civilization. We may live in cities and enjoy amazing comforts and technologies but our brains are still in the jungle.

Our prey instincts are alive and well in the deepest parts of our brains and personalities. These instincts are the root cause behind just about everything we do. They can explain why we behave the way we do. They hold the keys to the lives we have… and the lives we want. Let's take a closer look.

What's Eating Us?

Those poor monkeys just can't catch a break. Pythons attack them in the trees. Lions and tigers attack them on the ground and sometimes in the trees. Eagles can pluck a monkey off a branch. The harpy eagle in Panama makes its living by plucking monkeys off branches and eating them.

Soldiers use the term *combined arms* to describe an attack from all sides at once that leaves no room to run or hide. Monkey predators attack from ground, tree, and air. No monkey is ever truly safe no matter where it is. Humans evolved from monkeys. We therefore share that perilous legacy.

Birds hunted our ancestors. Thousands of monkey skulls have been found with holes and cuts caused by birds. A scientist named Lee Berger discovered a two-million-year old pre-human skull known as the Taung child with identical injuries. Berger concluded that our ancestors had to survive being hunted from both the ground and air. As he said, "Discoveries like this are key to understanding why we humans today view the world the way we do." We agree.

Getting Warmer

Discovering how to work with fire may be our single biggest technological advance. Fire in one form or another is responsible for just about every other technology we have. Look at the objects around you. Fire played a critical role in forming and distributing every single one of those objects.

Think about the many ways in which fire touches our lives. There is almost nothing more romantic than sitting by a fire. No camping trip is complete without a bonfire. What tastes better than flame-grilled food? Just about all of our energy comes from some kind of fire. Our computers run on energy. Our weapons use fire. Fire is everywhere.

Fire gives and takes life. Forest fires kill trees and animals but also let new life take hold. Some pinecones need fire to release seeds and renew the forest. Fire eats. It breathes. It cannot survive without fuel and oxygen. Some people describe fire as an animal. This description is not too far off.

The Ultimate Predator

What do you get when you cross a snake's body and scales, a big cat's legs and fangs, a bird of prey's wings and talons, and fire? You get a mythical creature that appears in just about every society on Earth. This terrible beast is a dragon. Dragons transcend time and culture. People have widely different beliefs, superstitions, and religions but everyone recognizes a dragon. Humans may have images of our predators wired into our physical brain circuits. Many cultures also see dragon slayers as superheroes.

Welcome to the Herd

A lone monkey cannot fight off a predator but a group of monkeys has a much better chance of coming out on top. A lone monkey has a one hundred percent chance of being attacked. A monkey in a group of twenty-five monkeys has only a four percent chance of being attacked. There is also strength in numbers that may allow the troop to defend itself without any casualties. It is no wonder that monkeys are social animals. The catch is that any effective group needs both teamwork and leadership.

Follow the Leader

Any manager can tell you that a bunch of individuals doing their own thing is not very effective at whatever they are trying to do. Getting them to work as a team requires a strong leader and hierarchy. Humans are social animals who function best in groups. We can develop serious mental and physical problems if isolated for too long. Leaders can exert amazing power over their groups to make them do things that no one person would do on their own.

The Importance of Fitting In

The science of rank theory says that depression may be a natural response to loss of rank. Depression eases the sting of losing and helps people cope with defeat. This prevents the loser from suffering further injury. It also helps preserve the group by lowering aggression and establishing a hierarchy. We see this as part of our prey legacy.

Humans will do almost anything to fit in with at least one group. Groucho Marx may have boasted that he would not join any club that would have him as a member but even he was not exactly a loner.

Prey Behavior

Prey animals behave very differently than predator animals. Prey tends to respond with fear and hesitation when placed in a new situation. Predators tend to respond with aggression. Prey cuts and runs. Predators stand firm. Prey animals hide and may even have guards looking out for the group. Predators sit out in the open because nobody is going to mess with them.

We believe that humans are prey animals and that everything we do comes from a place of not wanting to be killed and eaten. Our brains are wired with the images of our main predators that keep showing up in our myths and traditions. Our tribes and nations evolved from the need for protection against predators.

Putting It All Together

Seeing humans as prey animals who depend on core beliefs to avoid being killed and eaten is the key to understanding why so many of us don't have the joy and success we want in our lives. It is also the key to learning how to use those limits to our advantage.

You may not want to see yourself as a prey animal. We understand. We hope you understand that this seeming weakness can be the source of amazing power with the capacity to change your life forever.

The Enlightened Savage by Anthony goes into our evolutionary history, how it shapes who we are today, and what we can do about it in much more detail. You may also enjoy *The Natural Savage,* which goes into great detail about evolutionary science and what it means for us today.

* * *

Chapter 8: Understanding Core Beliefs

If our brains are like computer hardware then our thoughts, beliefs, and feelings are like software that depends on the brain to function. This chapter shows you how emotional programming generates the core beliefs that shape our lives.

Our brains are physically wired to interpret our core beliefs as survival programming that tells us who our predators are and how to avoid getting killed and eaten. This programming runs deep inside our brains. Most of us are only rarely aware of our core beliefs because the conscious mind is only a small part of everything happening inside our heads.

Identifying Your Mental Programming

Identifying your core beliefs is the first step in changing them. Your causes create your effects and your effects give you all the clues you need to expose the causes. It is therefore very easy to figure out what your core beliefs are. All you need to do is look at the results in all areas of your life.

These results are feeding a cycle of emotional addiction and continuing the cycle that keeps creating your reality. You are not experiencing your desired levels of wealth, happiness, joy, love, etc. because your responses directly tie to your core beliefs. Exposing your core beliefs requires self observation. We will talk about self observation more in Chapter 15.

You are a prey animal whose brain is designed for self-preservation and self-preservation only. Your conscious mind is literally doing little more than tagging along for the ride of its life. Millions of years of evolution have taught your brain that it must be right in order to carry out its mission of self-preservation. It will throw huge obstacles in your path whenever you try to break the addictive cycle you made for yourself.

Programming the Human Animal

Humans form most of our beliefs about how the world works as young children. Children do not have the mental skills of adults. Children younger than two years old don't even have a sense of self. They see themselves as one with the world. This is the perfect mental place from which to receive emotional survival programming because the brain has not yet developed barriers to learning.

These barriers start to form when the child develops a sense of "I" separate from her or his environment. The barriers act as firewalls that protect the core beliefs against change and become stronger over time. Primitive life was much simpler than modern life. People did not have the opportunities that most of us take for granted today. They had little reason to change and every reason to establish and stick to routines that kept them alive as long as possible.

Your brain interpreted your earliest emotions as survival instructions and built the programming that created your core beliefs. Your core beliefs are your deepest layers of mental software. They are your brain's operating system. Each layer of programming in our heads connects to and depends on the layers beneath it. We have less and less control over each layer as we go deeper but these deepest layers have the most control over us.

We cannot upgrade our physical brains but we can upgrade our mental software starting with our core beliefs.

Emotional Programming

Emotions may begin before birth. We saw in Chapter 4 that each emotion produces a set of chemicals that circulate throughout our entire bodies in our bloodstream. Medical studies show that people experiencing negative emotions actually make toxic chemicals inside their bodies. This means that negative emotions are literally poisonous! Positive emotions are harmless and even beneficial.

A mother experiencing negative emotions and making toxic chemicals may pass these poisons to her fetus. The fetus inside the womb may therefore be experiencing positive or negative emotions that will stick with her until she either changes them or dies.

Look around you. Why is the world full of sadness and angst? Negativity is everywhere and comes in thousands of forms. Why is there so much suffering in the world?

Remember that humans as prey animals. Prey animals are always in danger and must always be at least a little afraid. Waiting for something bad to happen is awful. Any soldier will tell you that the calm before the battle is often worse than the actual combat. This could explain why depression, stress, and worry are so common in humans.

Pregnant mothers are no exception. They may actually be more prone to emotional swings because of hormonal changes and the maternal drive to protect the young. The fetus may be soaking up this negativity while being unable to understand what is happening.

Children rely on emotions because they lack logic. The newborn child's brain immediately begins absorbing everything around him as survival instructions to keep him alive. Remember that humans have not adapted to civilization. Our brains are still in the middle of Africa surrounded by hungry lions, pythons, and eagles. The child has no choice but to learn to stay alive.

A person who is at one with their surroundings and who lacks the ability to analyze or question anything will probably accept everything they encounter as truth. This combination of openness and lack of sense of self allows children to learn fundamental lessons about how the world works and how they must behave in order to avoid being killed and eaten.

Children really are like sponges because they absorb everything without question. They do this in the form of emotional programming that forms core beliefs. Every person has core beliefs that direct our actions without any conscious thought. The sense of self that develops later protects these early core beliefs and the stage is set for the child to keep repeating the same general patterns again and again.

Building Belief Systems

A growing child starts to develop logic and rational thinking on top of his emotions. This leads him to form conclusions about his emotional programming that we call our core beliefs. We may or may not be aware of our beliefs but we interpret every one of them as "the truth." If an animal's parents shove the young into the burrow at noon then the youngster will learn to hide at midday. If a child's parents are abusive then the child may learn to be submissive.

Everyone has many experiences that impact us in different ways. Different experiences and patterns of experience eventually create different beliefs. This assortment of beliefs forms a system of beliefs that affects every single area of our lives. Some of our beliefs may even contradict other beliefs. We normally don't become aware of contradicting beliefs because they tend to form at different times and get triggered by different circumstances.

Having conflicting beliefs does not make us dishonest or mean that we lack integrity. All it means is that humans are far more emotional than logical. It is very difficult to be aware of a conflicting belief when one experiences a strong emotion.

How Beliefs Work

Core beliefs work like sunglasses. Sunglasses change incoming light before it hits our eyes. The world does not change. Only our perception changes. Wear sunglasses long enough and you will eventually forget you have them on. Core beliefs change how we see the world before we are aware of seeing anything. We carry our core beliefs from birth and are not normally aware that they are at work deep inside of us even when they are working against what we want in life.

The human brain contains a small area called the *Reticular Activation System* or RAS. The RAS is a group of cells that decides which information is important or not. Imagine walking through an airport not paying attention to the many announcements until you hear your flight being called. This is an example of the RAS at work.

The RAS decides which pieces of information you will be aware of out of the masses of information around you. You are only aware of a tiny bit of all that is happening behind you. One source says that your brain processes two hundred million bits of information for every single bit you are aware of. The RAS is a very effective filter. It is critical for survival because it separates things that might get you killed and eaten from everything else.

We automatically filter everything that happens to us according to core beliefs. Just about every belief, thought, and feeling we ever have throughout our lives is absolutely consistent with our core beliefs. Prey animals cannot afford to not follow their core beliefs. Humans are no exception. The top priority our brains have is to keep us from getting killed and eaten.

Staying Alive

Most children fear monsters that might leap out of the closet or from under the bed to get them. Many people fear things that go "bump" in the night. These things represent predators waiting to invade our refuges and attack us in our sleep. Our brains are wired to fear monsters and noises because that is what we had to do to survive.

Survival Habits

Humans of all ages establish and stick to routines no matter what. We take comfort in our routines. This makes perfect sense. For example, if a predator attacks at dusk then its prey should be out and about during the day and asleep out of reach at night. if a predator attacks at noon then the prey may want to be nocturnal. Sticking to this routine helps the prey stay alive.

Prey habits are all about avoiding predators. Humans are prey animals whose top priority is not getting killed and eaten. We therefore form habits to help us survive and then stick to those habits no matter how inconvenient, uncomfortable, or awful they are. We learned over countless generations that straying from our routine puts us at risk of being killed and eaten. Our brains do everything in their power to keep that from happening. This is why people refuse to change until the pain of not changing is worse than the pain of changing.

Imagine a gopher that hides from hungry birds during the day. Most gophers will not leave their burrows during the day unless some emergency happens. Flooding the burrow gives the gopher the choice of certain death by drowning or possible death by escaping. In this example, the risk of following the normal routine becomes greater than the risk of doing something different and the gopher will leave the burrow.

Humans work the same way except that many of our fears are based on past experiences or on future anticipations. They are not real. They are imagined.

The Comfort Zone

Our routines form our *comfort zone*. We refer to doing things we don't normally do as "leaving the comfort zone." How did you feel the last time you left your comfort zone? Maybe someone asked you to deliver a short speech to a group of your peers. You may have felt scared, nervous, insecure, and ready to bolt at a moment's notice. This is a perfect example of our prey instincts telling us to get back in our comfort zone as quickly as possible. The urge to get back to our comfort zone increases the farther we stray because we perceive the growing distance as danger.

This happens because our brains are wired to learn and follow habits designed to keep us alive. We do this by learning how our predators behave and then creating patterns to avoid them, even if our predators only exist in our imagination.

The comfort zone is nothing more or less than behavioral boundaries set by our core beliefs that form when we are too young to understand what is happening. Core beliefs form our entire reality from birth to death unless we take action to change them.

You can change your beliefs. The catch is that changing your beliefs will force you to confront programming that your brain interprets as being essential for your very survival. This is why crash diets, New Years' resolutions, joining a gym, opening a savings account, cutting up the credit cards, and other drastic changes rarely last more than a few days. At some point the desire for change surrenders to the brain's built-in attempts to keep you from getting killed and eaten.

What are some examples of drastic changes you have attempted in your own life? How have they worked out for you? Most importantly, how can one change when that runs up against instincts designed to keep us alive?

Act First, Ask Later

A prey animal needs to react to predators without question. Indecision causes hesitation. Hesitation gives predators an extra split second to move in for the kill. Groups of social animals suffer when predators get lucky because each loss increases the danger for everybody else.

Take a good look at any animal whose parents raise the young. The young stick around to learn the survival skills they need to stay alive. Prey animals learn when they can come out, where to go, how to avoid predators, and when to retreat back home. Survival depends on absorbing this information and mastering the skills without question. Questions lead to indecision and hesitation that could be fatal. One must act without question.

All Beliefs are False

The dictionary defines *belief* as, "the mental acceptance of and conviction in the truth, actuality, or validity of something." We see our beliefs as truth. Two plus two equals four because we believe it does. If you believe that two plus two equals five then no amount of argument will convince you otherwise

Beliefs equal truth because they are the mental sunglasses that filer our senses before we perceive the sensation. Your RAS selects which sensory input is important based on our beliefs. Our beliefs color every bit of that input. Only then do we become aware of the sensation.

If our personal reality is based on core beliefs then the universe that each of us experiences is not the cause but the effect of whatever is left over after our core beliefs do their work. The statement, "I'll believe it when I see it." is backward. We see things because we believe them within the limits of the laws of physics and waveforms. This has some amazing implications that we will explore in Appendix B.

We said it a few pages ago and will say it again: The truth is that all beliefs are false. Think of a belief you have and ask yourself whether it is true or whether it is something that you have decided is true. For example, you may believe that money is hard to earn while someone else believes it is easy. Which is true?

You formed your core beliefs from the emotional programming you received at a very young age. These beliefs shape your reality and everything in it. A belief is something that you have decided is true whether or not it really is true.

You may believe that it is cold outside and someone right beside you may believe it is quite comfortable. Each belief is true only to the person holding that belief. Neither belief has any objective reality because it only exists in the mind of the believer. Beliefs are all based on perception.

Core Beliefs in Action

Anthony really wanted a toy microscope when he was six years old. His parents were poor back then but his mother said she would gladly buy it for him. The she told Anthony that she could not buy it because there wasn't enough money for food. Anthony was angry because his mother had broken her promise. He confronted his mother but she insisted that she could not afford it.

Then Anthony's mother bought him the microscope. The toy that should have brought happiness instead brought incredible guilt because Anthony thought his parents had gone hungry. He vowed to never feel that guilt again and to buy himself every toy he could as soon as he could. That is exactly what he did in an effort to satisfy his inner six year old child.

Anthony was thirty five years old and deep in debt as a result of this core belief before he finally mentioned this incident to his mother. She was shocked. She told Anthony that she really wanted to buy the microscope but realized she would be short grocery money if she did. Then she got a small bonus in her paycheck and immediately bought the microscope.

Anthony's mother acted out of love and caring for his wants and needs but his young brain saw it as breaking a promise. That trivial incident affected Anthony for decades. It even stayed with him long after he thought he had finally let go of it.

Don't laugh. Everyone can probably tell a similar story about their own lives. What events helped shape your life and how could the truth be different from what you believe? Try talking to whoever else was involved in those incidents. What they tell you about how they interpreted things may be very different from what you believe.

Don't worry if you are unable to talk to these other people. Just ask yourself how you could interpret the exact same events differently. Can you think of a positive way to interpret something that you currently interpret negatively?

This exercise proves that all beliefs are false because some layers of reality are both subjective and personal. Your beliefs form your reality. Your personal reality may not have anything in common with anyone else's personal reality. Realizing this simple truth and letting it sink in can be incredibly liberating.

There's No Escape

Emotional programming creates core beliefs that color every bit of information our brains receive. These beliefs direct our every thought and action and create results that are perfectly compatible with the original programming. These beliefs create a self-fulfilling prophecy that becomes our comfort zone that helps us avoid being killed and eaten by predators… real or imagined.

Maybe you learned at an early age that your dreams and the things you love to do are bad or that you don't deserve them.

You will do everything in your power to keep from living your dreams or doing the things you love to do. This includes sabotaging yourself whenever it looks like you might be about to do those things.

A very talented young woman loved composing music and singing. She had great connections in the music industry and her career kept trying to take off only to crash and burn soon after she started leveraging opportunities. This kept on happening again and again. Meanwhile, she lived in poverty with barely enough money for instruments. She called her father every time it seemed like things were finally about to happen. The crash came soon after this call.

The father knew all about his daughter's love of music. He repeatedly punished her while she was growing up by putting all of her instruments on the sidewalk with a "Free" sign on them whenever she failed to live up to his exacting rules. This taught her that she was not worthy to live her lifelong dream of becoming a known musician.

The woman's prey brain sensed her pushing the edge of the comfort zone whenever her career showed signs of life. It responded by forcing her back into her comfort zone. She did not call her father to share the good news. She called him to feed her emotional addiction to not having the career she so desperately wanted and deserved.

Computer software depends on the hardware. Your brain is the hardware and your core beliefs are the deepest layer of software. Your brain interprets its core beliefs as survival instructions and does everything it can to follow those rules to the letter.

There is an old song that says you can't win, you can't break even, and you can't get out of the game. That's the bad news. The good news is that you can direct the game toward any outcome you want.

* * *

Chapter 9: The Cycle of Addiction

If a tree puts out fruit that is not fit to eat then we need to look at the roots of that tree to find the problem. Trying to fix the fruit itself won't accomplish anything. Good roots make good fruit. Bad roots make bad fruit. The physical world that we each see, hear, touch, smell, and taste is nothing but the fruit of our inner programming. If we don't like our worlds then we need to fix our roots. Our core beliefs are our roots.

We all have roots that need fixing. The problem is that our core beliefs trigger emotions that produce addictive chemicals that attach to every cell in our bodies. Each of us is literally addicted to a certain emotional pattern. Each of us is literally a junkie who will fight to the death to keep from kicking the habit.

Everyone who is addicted to a drug like heroin, crack, or meth knows how harmful those drugs are. They know the drugs are killing them. They know they shouldn't do it and will promise to quit every time they come down from their most recent high. These good intentions fade as soon as they start craving the next fix. Emotional addictions work the same way.

The only difference between you and someone addicted to street drugs is that your body is manufacturing its own drugs instead of getting them through pills, injections, or pipes. If you are a drug addict then you are addicted to both the emotional pattern that got you started on the drugs and the drugs themselves.

You are a junkie. Every single person is a junkie. Some of us are addicted to emotional patterns that lead to joy, fulfillment, and getting what we want. Most of us are addicted to emotional patterns that lead us away from what we want in life.

Think about everything that is going wrong in your life. It may seem hard to believe that you are physically addicted to being broke, unhappy, unhealthy, in relationship conflicts, etc. but that's exactly what's happening. Now imagine being just as addicted to being wealthy, happy, healthy, in a loving relationship, etc. You can never stop being an addict but you can change your addiction from negative to positive any time you want.

Feeding the Addiction

Every experience you had since birth (and possibly before) triggered an emotion. Good experiences trigger good emotions. Bad experiences trigger bad emotions.

For example, maybe your parents repeatedly told you that you would never amount to anything or that you would never measure up to your siblings. You looked up to and listened to your parents because your survival depended on it. Your young brain had no way to distinguish between meaningless disparagement and avoiding a hungry lion. All it knew is that your parents were the authorities who obviously knew how to stay alive.

Each reminder about your unworthiness triggered a raw emotion that sent waves of chemicals through your veins to the opiate receptors in each cell of your body. Each cell responds whenever a chemical docks with its designated receptors. Emotional states affect our entire bodies at a cellular level.

The emotional waves subsided and left feelings of sadness and inferiority in their wake. Nobody likes feeling this way so you did the natural thing and buried those feelings. Burying feelings may keep them out of sight but they are not out of mind. Build up enough buried feelings and you will start to think thoughts such as, "I really must be worthless," or, "I need to act in this manner because it is the only way my parents will pay attention to me."

This is how emotions become beliefs. Beliefs are your truth. You are now addicted to this emotional pattern and the chemicals it produces. Your brain uses these core beliefs to rationalize and justify taking action to keep feeding this addiction such as the young woman we met in Chapter 8 who called her abusive father every time her music career showed signs of life.

If you see yourself as anything less than fully worthy of the life you want then your emotions will play right along. Those emotions may be awful but you will stick with them because they are your response to your survival instructions. Your addiction to these emotions will keep you coming back for more.

Feelings whisper to us about what is right and wrong to do. They help keep us from leaving our comfort zone by making us afraid whenever we step outside that self-made box. Our emotions literally lead us around like faithful puppy dogs.

Anthony once spoke with a woman during a coaching session who said that she wanted to marry a wonderful man and raise children in a nice house. This woman was a prostitute at the time. Her actions prevented her from getting what she wanted. Her core beliefs made her feel unworthy to the point where she did everything possible to avoid getting what she wanted. She followed her survival instructions exactly as written.

If most of our problems exist because our brains are following their survival instructions then there may be nothing wrong with us. The bad things in our lives may be happening because we are perfectly OK! We will explain this more in Chapter 10.

Bridging the Gap

Emotional programming creates thoughts that justify the need for more similar emotions and lock us into a pattern of addiction. This addiction compels us to take any action necessary to keep getting regular doses of addictive emotional chemicals.

Actions bridge the gap between ourselves and the outer world. Every action causes a result.

Experiencing the result creates an emotion that reinforces the original experience and makes it even stronger. No amount of sheer effort, positive thinking, or trying to use the Law of Attraction will help. Trying to use the Law of Attraction can actually make the addiction worse because it lets you think you are making changes when in fact nothing of the sort is happening. The Law of Realization demonstrates that relying on the Law of Attraction bends the waveform in a way that makes repeating the same old cycle even more likely.

For example, if you believe that you are not worthy of being married to a great guy and raising kids in a nice house then you will do all you can to keep that guy from marrying you. Being a prostitute is a great way to make sure that no family-minded man will choose you as a wife. It fulfills negative core beliefs by keeping the marriage and children from coming true. The conscious goal of wanting marriage and children exists to serve the unconscious goal of fulfilling core beliefs about being unworthy.

The results validate our core beliefs. The cycle is complete. Around we go again and again and again and again and again.

Raising the Stakes

Start taking an addictive drug. A small dose will give a nice high at first but the user will soon begin needing higher and higher doses to get the same high. Trying to stop using the drug puts the body into withdrawal because it has become addicted to the drug. Addiction means that the body needs that drug to function normally. This is why withdrawal can be a long, painful, and even dangerous process.

Emotional chemicals work the same way. Experience the same emotion often enough and your body will become addicted to the chemicals that emotion produces. You will become a junkie to your emotions. Your brain will do everything it can to feed that addiction and will justify doing this based on the core beliefs that are its survival instructions.

You will need increasing doses of emotional chemicals over time to maintain the same effect. This explains why people tend to experience escalating patterns over time. Someone who goes through up and down financial cycles may keep making more money when things are good only to fall into increasingly dire straits when times are tough.

Think about your own life. What is your emotional pattern? How have the stakes increased over time?

Symptoms of Negative Addiction

Are you living your ideal life right now? Be honest. If not then what is holding you back? Here are some examples:

- Are you afraid of digging yourself into a deeper financial hole?
- Do you keep quiet because you worry about getting tongue-tied at a critical moment?
- Do you avoid money-making opportunities because they sound too good to be true or because you think they won't work out?
- Does financial freedom seem to be totally out of reach based on repeated experience?
- Do you worry about what others might think of you if you do something different?
- Do you sometimes spend days rehashing something that happened and wondering how it would have worked out if only you'd made a different decision?
- Do you keep your good ideas to yourself because you think people will put you down?

- Are you afraid that you will repeat a past mistake or bad decision?
- Do you keep picking the same type of abusive person despite wanting a loving, healthy, passionate relationship?
- Do you sometimes feel that you are not in control of your emotions?
- Have you ever felt like giving up because you believe that nothing you can do will change your situation?
- Have you been trying to use the Law of Attraction with little or no measurable results?

If you said yes to any of these questions then you are most probably caught in a negative addictive cycle that is affecting every area of your life either directly or indirectly. Some of the symptoms of a negative addiction include watching yourself doing things you know you should not do or holding back from doing the things you should do out of fear, worry, or doubt. Going through things like this repeatedly is another clear sign of a negative addiction.

The most painful part of experiences like this is convincing yourself that, "This time will be different!" despite knowing full well that you are doing the same old thing yet again. The same old result happens again and leaves you knowing that you were the one who procrastinated until it was too late, dated the same type of person yet again, felt too scared to ask for what you want, etc. You know deep down that you alone are responsible for the life you are living whether you like it or not.

Each time leaves you wanting to do things differently from now on but without the ability or knowledge to change. Every person goes through this at least once in their lives. Talk about frustrating! No one ever said being a junkie is easy.

Mental Pollution

Say you want to go into business making fine furniture. You need a building and some equipment. You also need a set of blueprints with the designs of what you want to build. Raw materials such as wood, glue, pegs, nails, paint, and varnishes are also essential as is a place to store your finished products. You assemble everything you need and go to work making furniture.

Sawing the wood creates sawdust and wood scraps that drop on the floor. Sanding each piece creates more dust that falls to the floor. You put on the finish coat of varnish and drop the empty bucket on the floor.

What happens if you never clean up the waste? All would be well at first because you could simply sidestep the mess. Keep going and you would eventually have to walk on it. Keep deferring the cleaning and production would slow down as you start tripping over the waste. You would eventually become unable to function and go out of business.

What emotional waste and addictions are you carrying in your mind that serve no positive purpose? What happens as your brain becomes overloaded with programs that need to be deleted for you to move forward?

We mentioned in Chapter 9 that many of us choose to put off or bury feelings that might cause pain or discomfort. This seems easy because our conscious mind soon forgets about these feelings just like you may sometimes forget about a bit of sawdust that falls on the floor. Each buried or deferred feeling is like a bit of sawdust or an empty varnish can waiting for you to pick it up. You have a clump of sawdust for every person you have not forgiven. You have an empty varnish can for every unresolved emotional hurt. It adds up over time.

Every unresolved experience in our lives remains inside our brains. The sheer amount of accumulated garbage forces us to deal with it automatically based on past programming. There is so much clutter that we lose track of what to do or what needs cleaning first. We respond by putting off until later the things we don't want to deal with. Our brains slowly build up a large collection of unresolved experiences that take up space and affect how we feel.

A salesperson making a call may be hanging on to past refusals from previous calls. He sees the current call through the filter of those prior rejected calls. Does hanging on to those calls help or hinder making an effective call that ends in a sale? We know that it hinders because the new call is made from a place of fear that increases the odds of receiving yet another refusal.

Someone may enter a new relationship hoping it will be better than the last one. She may be hanging on to the hurt from the last relationship to avoid making the same mistake again. She sees the new relationship through the filters she built about her last experience of pain or failure. Doing that actually increases the odds that the new relationship will turn out like the old one.

Many people turn to the Law of Attraction because it sounds easy. They think that cleaning the factory is as easy as putting away the broom and dustpan, thinking clean thoughts, and imagining a sparkling clean factory to make all the clutter vanish.

Whatever we project into the world increases the chances that the projection will come true. This may sound like the Law of Attraction but it is actually the Law of Realization. Everything you think, feel, and do alters the waveform and what is likely to happen.

Projecting the desire for a clean factory won't work for the same reason that you should not expect to manifest a single hundred-dollar bill any time soon. In this example, what you are really projecting is laziness because you don't want to roll up your sleeves and do the work.

If you don't take action to clean your factory then your factory will remain clogged with garbage. If you don't take active steps to clear unresolved experiences from your mind then your mind will hang on to those experiences.

Every trip around the cycle of addiction leaves more buried feelings scattered about. Buried feelings pollute your mind just like drugs or emotional chemicals pollute the body. Clearing this pollution requires you to roll up your mental sleeves and take action. No amount of wishing away your abusive parent, trying to get the bank to accept your overdue credit card bill as a check made out to you, or waiting for Mr. or Mrs. Right to spontaneously ring your doorbell will make any of it go away.

Thankfully there is a very easy way to free yourself from all this baggage.

* * *

Chapter 10: Redefining Success

You are a prey animal living in perpetual fear of getting killed and eaten and have become addicted to negative emotions and patterns. You may be wondering just what the heck is wrong with you to have gotten yourself into this mess. That's a natural reaction but we would like to ask you a different question: What if you are perfectly OK?

Let us be more specific: What if the fact that you are not living your perfect life and are addicted to negative emotions is not happening because something is wrong with you but because your brain is perfectly healthy and working perfectly well?

You May Be OK

Imagine ten identical computers in perfect working order. Nine computers have Program A installed. The tenth has Program B installed. Program A is great for helping users get lots of work done. Program B does nothing but crash and cause problems all the time.

It should be obvious that the tenth computer is not the problem. The program is crashing because it is a bad program. The computer is carrying out its instructions to the letter. The letters themselves are the problem.

If we define success in terms of expectations and meeting goals then Program A is a success and Program B is a failure. This is how most of us normally define success and failure.

If we define success as how well the computer executes the program then both programs are equally successful. Program B is made to crash and is doing just that. How and why Program B was built to crash does not matter. The code is bad, period.

Your brain has been following your core beliefs to the letter throughout your entire life. It will keep following that programming until you either die or act to change that programming. You are successfully following your beliefs and creating your reality based on those beliefs.

If your program is set for wealth and happiness then your life is rich and happy. If your program is set for frustration and defeat then you are living a tough life. Either way, you are absolutely successful!

Let's go back to the tenth computer with the lousy program. What do you think would happen if we removed Program B and installed Program A? We already know that the computer is working perfectly so we can safely predict that it will run Program A just as well as the other nine computers. The computer has not changed. Only the programming has changed.

Program A is a great program. The tenth computer will start doing the same thing that the other nine computers have been doing all along because the hardware is working perfectly. The bad program is the problem because the computer has no choice but to follow its programming. The fact that the tenth computer is identical to the other nine means that it can run the good program just as well.

The fact that your life does not have all the wealth and happiness you want may well mean that your brain is working properly. All you have to do is change your programming. The fact that you are not living your ideal life is probably a good thing when you look at it this way!

We cannot say for sure that this is true in all situations because the brain is an organ that can malfunction just like any other organ. Just be open to the possibility that there may be a lot less wrong with you than you think. You may be perfectly OK and only need to change programs. That's a pretty encouraging thought, isn't it?

Failure Does Not Exist

Both Jim and Anthony know about therapy and counseling. We have also tried many different self-help programs to figure out why we felt so crazy and why we kept ending up in the same place over and over again. Most of all, we kept wondering why dealing with our inner fears, anxieties, and other psychological challenges was so exasperatingly difficult.

We finally realized that we were attacking symptoms instead of dealing with the actual problem. Anyone who makes a mistake or comes up against something that isn't working the way they want takes steps to solve the problem. For example, if your car gets a flat tire your first instinct will be to patch the tire.

Many of us fix our inner tires with layer upon layer of patches only to wonder why we are experiencing yet another flat. We keep applying patches without realizing that the real problem is not the tire but the road strewn with nails and potholes.

This is a great example of the cycle of addiction that we talked about in Chapter 9. Our programmed beliefs keep us driving down the same road fixing the same tires over and over again. We keep making the same mistakes. Every patch leaves the tire a little weaker and a little more likely to blow out when we can least afford it.

All of the self-help, motivation, and Law of Attraction in the world cannot and will not fix the road. All they can do is slap on yet one more patch, pump yet more air, and send us out to drive yet another lap and go back through the same old cycle on the same old destructive road.

Pulling over again and again to keep fixing the same tire gets old and exhausting yet we keep patching and pumping and patching and pumping because we forget that solving the problem is as easy as turning off the bad road.

Staying on the road is a perfectly successful way to make sure that we will keep patching and pumping. Turning off the road is a perfectly successful way to make sure that we can finally stop patching and pumping. Either path is successful. The only variable is how we define success.

Not turning off the bad road means that we define success as patching and pumping. Turning off the road means that we define success as not patching and pumping. There really is no such thing as failure. What about you? What are you succeeding at doing or not doing? How well does this success match what you would like to be doing or not doing?

Don't Sweat the Small Stuff

The number of stars in the Milky Way galaxy we live in is greater than the number of neurons in your brain. The number of galaxies in the universe is greater than the number of neurons in your brain. The Milky Way itself is about 100,000 light years across, which means that it would take us 100,000 years to get from one side to the other traveling at 186,000 miles per second (the speed of light).

Our sun and solar system is a tiny speck compared to all of this. The sun itself is more than a million times larger than the Earth by volume. The distance around the world at the equator is about twenty two million times your height. Think about this for a moment and then ask yourself whether your problems are really anything big.

Everyone receives a ration of what we can call life energy at birth. Everyone dies when this energy is used up. You get to choose how to use that energy while you are alive. Think about your problems again. How many of them are really worth using up even a drop of your precious life energy?

Here is a very simple example: Say you're driving down the freeway at seventy miles per hour on your way to an appointment five miles away. You are on track to arrive on time when suddenly someone cuts you off and slows you down to fifty five. What do you do? Do you let yourself get uptight and upset at the other driver?

Slowing to fifty five will cost you seventy seconds but these seventy seconds are not the issue. The real issue is the amount of life energy you spent on your frustration at being unable to control the other driver. Your frustration created negative emotions that created poisons that affected every cell in your body. This burned up your life energy. Accepting the situation and perhaps even allowing yourself to enjoy the extra minute of peace could generate positive emotions.

Stop yourself whenever you feel yourself becoming angry, frustrated, sad, upset, afraid, etc. and ask yourself whether the situation is really worth your life energy or whether it's just something small that's just not worth getting all riled up about.

Take another look at the size comparisons on the previous page and you will see that everything is small stuff. Dr. Richard Carlson was right when he said, "Don't sweat the small stuff… and it's all small stuff!"

Taking Stock

If you can…

- Get to the point where you realize that you are perfectly OK,
- Understand that you have been absolutely successful in life even if you have only managed to get what you don't want, and
- Stop worrying about things that just aren't worth being worried about (which is just about everything)

... then you will open yourself up to taking the kind of action that will take you in the right direction by altering the waveform to make what you want more likely to occur than not. In other words, you will be taking steps to consciously realize what you want instead of unconsciously realizing what you don't want.

Doing this is not as difficult as you might think.

Chapter 11: Common Addictive Patterns

We bet that you have been there and done that. You have tried your utmost to get what you want in life by working longer hours, learning more, and putting out sheer effort. You have crawled, pushed, and shoved your way through the growing piles of sawdust and varnish cans in your factory to keep cranking out furniture at all cost. It's exhausting!

Why not simply let go of whatever is keeping you from what you wanted? Success and happiness has very little to do with effort and struggle and very much to do with cleansing yourself of old beliefs, habits, and emotions. Trying to be happy and successful without this cleansing process is like trying to make beautiful furniture in a filthy factory or drive while standing on the brake pedal. Doesn't work too well, does it?

It is also like trying to be happy and productive while addicted to an extremely toxic drug. Remember the cycle of addiction? Any difficulty you are having in getting and keeping what you want in life is a direct result of your addiction to your current counterproductive patterns. Drugs like heroin and meth are not their users. The pattern you are addicted to is not "you" but the remnants of past experiences.

Each of our inner obstacles is layered and interconnected with every other obstacle just like every bit of sawdust in our imaginary furniture factory is connected to every other bit of sawdust. For example, you may be conditioned to believe that life is hard and respond to easy times by making things hard for yourself. Does this sound familiar?

This belief may stem from a deep-rooted fear that you are not and will never be good enough. You try harder and harder to crack this belief by brute force, which feeds your belief that life is hard. Achieving your goal may seem satisfying but deep down it's the worst thing that could happen because you feel unworthy!

The fact that something came easy took you out of your comfort zone and your prey brain will do anything it can to get you back inside your burrow even if that means sabotaging your success. This feeds both your unworthiness addiction and your struggle addiction and the cycle begins again with yet another set of buried feelings to its credit.

This example may or may not describe your situation but we think you get the general idea. Negative addictive cycles are crazy-making. The sooner you can start breaking any negative addictions you have, the better.

Here is a look at some of the most common negative emotional patterns that people tend to be addicted to. We labeled them according to common feelings because that is the quickest and easiest way for you to decide whether one or more of these patterns describe your own life.

Read through this list and see how many of them make sense to you. It does not matter how many or how few of these patterns you have in your life. What matters is the effect they have on you, how extra much life energy they force you to consume, and how they keep you getting what you want in life.

Constant Fear and Anxiety

Many of us are slaves to our fears and worries. We spend so much time fearing that something might happen that we actually go out of our way to make it happen. Focusing a lot of attention on something that frightens us is a great way to make it happen. For example, if you are scared of dogs then dogs are more likely to bark at you or even attack you because dogs can literally smell the chemicals produced by your fear.

Have you ever:

- Worried about going deeper into debt and found yourself there in a matter of months?
- Feared that the pile of money you just earned will soon vanish and watched your bank account dwindle?
- Gone home knowing that another heated argument with your spouse or partner would ensue and gotten into that fight the moment you walked in the door?

Jim once suggested to a friend that he let go of the idea that his co-worker was manipulative and hard to get along with. After some effort, he "gave it a try." For the first time ever, his co-worker was pleasant all day!

This is not the Law of Attraction but belief filtering how you interpret events. The man with the manipulative coworker interpreted everything that person did as manipulative whether or not they intended it that way. Replacing that filter with one that saw the coworker as a decent person made Jim's friend interpret his coworker's actions as pleasant. He also acted more pleasant toward that person. Taking this action changed everything.

Changing yourself changes people around you. Try to control how someone will act and you will face stiff resistance. Interact with someone in a way that makes clear how you expect them to act and they will often meet your expectations. Let go of the need to control the other person and there will be nothing to resist. Let go of your expectations about the other person and they will be far more likely to pleasantly surprise you.

Interpreting what your spouse or partner says as an attack is a great way to get into a fight. Choosing to be peaceful lets you sidestep any attack or even see that what you thought was an attack is really a plea for attention or love.

Learning to understand the belief that triggers fear, anxiety, worry, or doubt helps you simply let go of that belief. This lets you lose the associated emotions and you will interpret the exact same events in a completely new way. The events will happen but they will stop triggering your fears. You will eventually learn that all conflict is really self-conflict.

This simple lesson alone has made miraculous changes in the lives of tens of thousands of people around the world.

Frustration, Anger, and Resentment

Life can be frustrating. People sometimes do things that really tick you off or even hurt you. It is only natural to let anger and frustration get the better of you sometimes or even to hold a grudge. The only problem with this is that you are the one who gets hurt. Your negative emotions cannot hurt anyone but you.

Jim tells the story of a woman at one of his seminars who told him that she could not live her ideal life because her father had verbally abused her. Jim asked her where her father is and learned that he had been dead for several years. Jim then asked, "So who is abusing you now?" It took the woman a few minutes to realize that she was abusing herself. This realization helped her let go of her negative core beliefs about her father and replace them with newer, more positive programming.

The word "happened" is the key. The event is over. All of the woman's anger and resentment cannot possibly hurt her dead father. What about you? What past events are you still angry about? What old frustrations do you carry with you? Who do you resent? Do you really think any of this is affecting the other person? Do you really think your frustration over being unable to have the money you want is helping you actually make that money? Hint: Probably not!

This logic works in the present moment as well. Say you are in a heated argument with someone. Who will win? The merits of the argument don't matter at all. Nobody ever wins any argument. We argue because we want to be right and to force our beliefs on someone else, forgetting that all beliefs are false. The fact that our beliefs form our truth says nothing about how someone else views them. Their beliefs form their truths.

What about your anger, frustration, and resentment? Is any of it bending the waveform toward or away from what you want? What are these negative emotions helping make real? Any feeling or belief you have is either moving you toward or away from what you want.

We absolutely guarantee that your frustration, anger, or resentment isn't getting you what you want. Let it go and move on.

Reliving the Past

Have you experienced any or all of the following?

- A bad business deal?
- Being hurt by someone you love?
- Not getting a deserved refund?
- Unexpected charges or fees?
- Something you said or did that you wish had gone differently, such as thinking of a witty comeback too late?
- Fraud or deception?

Bad things happen to good people. Everyone goes through things like this sometimes. The difference is that some of us let these incidents pass over us like water off a ducks' back and keep going with our lives while others hang onto and keep reliving them.

For example, you may not trust your current partner because your last partner cheated on you. Does hanging on to this infidelity help or hurt your current relationship? Are you opening yourself up to a loving relationship by treating your partner like a cheater? The same questions apply to every event you keep reliving even if that event was positive.

Hanging on to a negative event taints every new opportunity. Hanging on to a positive event makes it impossible to enjoy the present on its own merits because you will compare it to the past and probably find ways in which your current experience is not as good or satisfying as the past. Either way, you can't possibly get ahead if you keep thinking about and reliving the past.

It is fine and even necessary to learn from past experiences. Just don't bring that past into the present.

Loss of Control

Anything can happen at any time and it often does. We each have far less control over most of our lives than we can ever comfortably admit. Trying to hard to control things only leaves one feeling out of control because what you try to control ends up controlling you. The need for control removes your ability to be in control. Letting go of the need for control puts you firmly in control.

Anthony was constantly on the phone with realtors, inspectors, lenders, and others during the process of buying his first house. Issues came up one after another and the entire transaction dragged on and seemed like it might collapse. Finally, Anthony told his realtor that she was a professional who knew her job and to go ahead and do it. He then put the phone down and quit worrying. Three days later, all the pieces fell into place and Anthony moved in.

What things are you desperately trying to control in your own life? Maybe you just can't seem to lose weight or are stuck in a rut of losing the weight only to gain it right back again. Diets don't work and your weight seems to be in everyone's control but your own.

Maybe you feel like a piece of driftwood at your job. Your boss does not see how good you are, you get passed over for promotions, and people ignore you when you apply for better jobs. Again, you feel like you have no control over your job or your future.

Maybe you feel like you don't have any control in your relationship or in the dating world. Your marriage is in constant conflict no matter how hard you try (if you are married) or you just can't get past the second date (if you are single). Maybe you have brought yet another jerk into your life. Maybe your sex life is somewhat less than satisfying.

Each of these situations can leave a person feeling frustrated and completely out of control of her or his own life.

The key is to remember that all conflict is self-conflict. Your perceived need for control has nothing to do with any lack of control at all. All of these situations are happening because you are holding on to false beliefs about yourself or your situation. Stuff happens. That much nobody can control. What we can do is refuse to let these experiences tie us down so that we can look at every new situation with fresh eyes.

That, dear reader, is real freedom.

We will discuss control more in Chapter 12.

Confusion and Distraction

Can't decide which way is up? Having trouble finding your life's purpose? Feeling lost and confused?

Steve did pretty well at whatever he tried. He was good at a lot of things but not exceptional at anything. He therefore struggled to move beyond a moderate income or mid-level job and would often say things like, "If only I'd kept at it a little longer," "If only I'd started this 10 years ago," or "If only I had another shot at it."

Steve attended many life-purpose seminars and came out all pumped up and excited at finally having the clarity he needed. This clarity soon faded and left him still trying to figure out just what his mission in life was.

Then one day he realized that he was replaying his father's life. He finally let go and broke his addiction to mediocrity by losing his father's belief that success requires struggle. Steve's core belief that success requires struggle was completely unconscious. He internalized it so thoroughly that he could not see it.

What do the patterns and themes in your own life say about core beliefs you may hold in your own unconscious? How might losing these beliefs impact your life?

Chapter 12: The Need for Control

All of the patterns we discussed in the previous chapter stem from a single fundamental need, which is the need to control. Attempting to manipulate the world, our business affairs, relationships, other people, and other situations is the number one source of suffering.

We all need to feel like we're in control of our lives and our environments. We like to believe that there is such a thing as security and that we can bend the forces of nature to our will. Losing control is a very scary feeling.

You can use your resources to obtain the results you seek or to obtain other resources along the way. For example, you can buy things or persuade others to see your point of view. You can choose how to interpret things that happen to you. You can indeed control yourself. You can also wield some external influence. You also have far less control over your environment than you think you do. The trick is to recognize what you can and cannot control.

You Have Little Control

Accepting your near-total lack of control over your life is the first step to letting go of the need for control. For example, accepting the fact that you cannot control what people think of you is the first step to letting go of the need to be someone you are not and find people who will accept you for who you are.

People hurt other people. Everyone can probably recite a laundry list of people who have hurt them. We forget that we created the pain by choosing to let those people hurt us. We develop complex patterns to try and avoid the pain. We start judging others. We form opinions about everything and everyone we feel might hurt us. We see ourselves as victims and do all in our power to take control and avoid future hurts.

All of this effort actually weakens what little control we have. Our obsession with not getting hurt removes us from the moment and lets our life pass us by as we focus on our needs and live a scarcity-based life as a result. This is a perfect example of a negative addiction!

You always have just the amount of control you need and that is always far less than you think you need. Learn what you can control and forget about everything else. It's silly to try to control something that is beyond your control. You cannot be responsible for anything beyond your control.

If there is an action you can take, let go of the need to control the outcome and then take action. Just don't let yourself feel the need to control the outcome. If there is no action you can take, then simply let go and have the courage to leave it at that. Never forget that all you can do is influence probabilities by bending the waveform. This means that you can never get everything you want whenever you want it. You cannot "wish it" into existence. The Law of Attraction does not work.

Let Go of Control

Letting go of the need to control is like sailing, surfing, skiing, or even living your life to the fullest. It requires a subtle blend of control through skill and knowledge while allowing yourself to go with the flow. Remember that whatever you try to control will always end up controlling you.

Get clear about what you want and don't want. Create your vision for your ideal life. Take action for the things you can control and don't even bother trying for anything else. The results will astound you. Again, this is not about attraction or manifesting or putting on a happy face. It is about setting down your emotional baggage and liberating yourself from that burden.

Most people try to "keep it together" by suppressing emotions instead of simply letting them go. The perceived need to suppress our emotions creates the need for control. Someone who does not suppress their feelings can be labeled "out of control" and evicted from whatever group or groups she or he may belong to. Our fundamental need for control stems from an even deeper need for acceptance.

Need implies lack. If you need acceptance then you feel unaccepted. If you need control then you feel out of control. This makes perfect sense. For example, how can you need milk if you have a full carton in the fridge? The need only begins when the carton runs low.

You have far less control over your life than you think. You cannot control what will happen next. Remember that quantum physics only gives probabilities. All you can do is change the odds. You cannot control what other people think of you. You cannot control decisions made by others. So why worry about it?

Letting go of the need for control is what puts you in control and keeps you there. The choice not to need to control something keeps you in full control of your thoughts, feelings, emotions, and behaviors that are the only things you can ever hope to control. This is not the same as giving up control. The only thing you give up is trying to exert your control over things you can never control in an effort to make things turn out as you want them.

Conscious Observation

The key is to learn to distinguish between those things we can control and those we cannot. In other words, learn to identify the difference between controllable and uncontrollable circumstances. This requires becoming self-observant. Ask yourself often, "Is this action I am about to take moving me in the direction I want to go?" If not, don't take it. Stop and re-think the situation.

Becoming a "mind-full" observer lets you see situations clearly and gives you the opportunity to choose to let go of your need to control those situations. You can always choose not to burn up your allotment of life energy on something that is beyond your control. More importantly, you can take action to change your situation from a place of resourcefulness instead of lack. We will talk more about self observation in Chapter 15.

Chapter 13: The Power of Letting Go

Each of the examples in Chapter 11 involves non-resourceful beliefs and the equally non-resourceful emotions and feelings those beliefs trigger. We call them *non-resourceful* because they hinder your ability to live the life you want by draining your limited life energy.

It's Up to You

You alone carry your beliefs and you alone are addicted to your current emotional cycle. The responsibility is all yours and nobody else's. It is important that you acknowledge your absolute responsibility for your own cycle of addiction.

It is equally important that you avoid the temptation to beat yourself up for having these non-resourceful things inside you. Letting go of your old addiction should be a guilt-free process. Your non-resourceful beliefs, emotions, feelings, and actions are not enemies. They are survival instructions that performed beautifully. They kept you alive and brought you to this point. They formed because your brain did exactly what it is designed to do. Be happy you have them!

Our inner voices always whisper to us. The whispers can be loving and compassionate or negative. Listen to the loving and compassionate whispers and dismiss the negative whispers as fragments of who you used to be instead of accepting them as who you are today. You must see your past with love and compassion instead of anger and resentment if you want to make positive change.

Never let the past dictate your life today. Do the best you can without worrying whether it's good enough. Just remember that every present moment is always brand new. The past is over and done with. It is not happening to you anymore unless you let it keep happening.

We know we need food, clothing, shelter, water, sunlight, and oxygen to sustain life while often forgetting that we also need love to survive. Non-loving feelings are non-resourceful by nature. We saw in Chapter 4 that non-resourceful feelings actually create poisons that can threaten our very lives. Carrying around non-resourceful feelings is nothing more than a slow way to die a very painful death.

Letting go of a non-resourceful feeling changes your body chemistry and brain cells for the better. Keep letting go and the real you will begin to appear. This is the you who is full of joy, happiness, self-confidence, and peace of mind.

Try something today: Allow every unplanned experience, mishap, non-resourceful thought, or unwanted feeling and emotion to come over you as it happens. Let it live a life of its own for a short time. Then release it to become free-flowing energy once again. See your life through the knowledge that everything from thoughts and emotions to thunder and lightning has its own birth, life, and death. The only reason our painful past still exists is because we refuse to let it die a natural death by letting it go.

You do not need to let go of things that no longer support you. On the other hand, you do not need to live with pain and disappointment. Letting go of non-resourceful beliefs, emotions, and feelings is about nothing more than ending the pain and disappointment in your life. Carrying pain and disappointment tilts every waveform you interact with against you. Letting go tips the waveform in your favor. Letting go of what you want increases the odds that what you want will actually happen.

For example, if you are scared of dogs then the chance that a dog will bark at you goes up because dogs can sense fear. Letting go of the fear increases the chances that the same dog will either ignore you or be friendly.

Action is the key. Action is what moves Helen closer to the hamburger in the example we saw in Chapter 5. It does not matter if she wants the hamburger or how she feels about the hamburger. All she needs to do is keep moving toward the hamburger to get it. This is why we keep telling you that your beliefs and intentions don't matter nearly as much as you think they do.

Easy and Difficult

Here are a few things you probably already know:

- You probably know far more than the average person about how to let go just from the examples you already saw in this book.
- You may even know more about letting go than some people who have studied psychology or gone through all the self-help manuals out there.
- You are an expert at letting go but it isn't working for you the way you wish it would because you feel like something is holding you back.

You don't need any more tricks or methods. You have that part down. The real problem is bigger, more intensely personal, and more difficult to face. Tackling and defeating this problem will free you to succeed with money, relationships, and everything else you may want in your life.

You should know from Chapter 3 that the Law of Attraction is not going to work. Your problems won't vanish on their own. No amount of visualization, happiness, or gratitude will make the pieces fall into place. Most people go their entire lives without ever handling their issues and achieving the success they want and deserve. This can happen to you… or you can take action to make your personal freedom real.

Many people have a true desire to fulfill their deep-rooted and quite human needs for financial security, safety, love, and happiness but their core beliefs hold them back. People believe that they cannot have what they want, don't deserve them, are incapable of attaining them, or are somehow flawed to where their dreams can never come true.

Beliefs born of prey survival instincts keep the happiness, prosperity, or love people want just out of reach no matter how hard they struggle or how much they want it. Worse, these same beliefs force them to sabotage whatever good things come their way in order to feed their emotional addictions that come from the same survival instinct.

Getting past this by breaking out of your negative addictions and into more positive addiction is so simple and easy that anyone can do it. It is also incredibly complex and difficult to do if you don't know how. You already know this and would already be where you want to be if letting go were easy.

Why Letting Go Works

Let's recap the cycle of addiction we discussed in Chapter 9 to understand why letting go works. Our brains remember and interpret every early emotional experience as survival instructions designed to keep us alive in a jungle full of hungry predators. We attach the emotions we felt at the time with particular experiences. These early emotions form core beliefs as our logic and sense of "I" develops and we interpret our beliefs as truth. The emotional addictions behind our core beliefs drive us to take actions that cause results that we interpret through the lenses of our beliefs.

When confronted with a new situation, your mind attempts to make sense of it by scanning for similar experiences. It finds these similar experiences and brings up the attached feeling such as fear, regret, etc. Your brain looks for ways to get rid of the pain of unpleasant feelings and jumps to a quick conclusion about what you should think or how you should act. Your brain then justifies that conclusion by pulling in evidence from past experiences to support the conclusion as a self-protective survival response.

This means that your action is based on prior experiences that could be years or even decades old. All of this happens in an instant before your logical or rational mind can possibly think things through. Repeating the cycle over and over again for any experience strengthens the circuits in your brain that equate things like "money" and "hard to get." This happens again and again because you are addicted to the emotional patterns these cycles cause.

Old experiences and the associated emotional addictions control the vast majority of your current action. You may think that you are thinking things through and responding to the present situation in the present but all you are doing is making an excuse for going around the same old cycle yet again. Every junkie knows this process all too well and every single person on the planet is a junkie whether we realize it or not.

Letting go of your old emotions and feelings breaks the cycle of addiction and lets you truly live in the present. Over time, you form new emotional addictions. The difference is that this cycle of addiction revolves around positive emotions that improve your life and health instead of negative emotions that slowly poison you to death.

You are and will always remain a junkie addicted to emotional cycles. The question is whether you want to remain addicted to negative emotions or switch to something a little more uplifting.

The Benefits of Letting Go

You will see immediate results when you begin letting go, such as:

- Improved self-esteem and confidence that will help you in any situation
- Finding ways to start living the life you were meant to live
- Reducing and eventually eliminating your emotional stumbling blocks
- Eliminating the "need to please" that comes from desperate attempts to gain acceptance from others
- Putting yourself in the driver's seat of your own life
- Experiencing less depression or sadness in your life while experiencing more happiness and joy
- Quieting chronic stress and anxiety
- Never again needing to read another self-help book or attend another seminar
- Replacing destructive habits with constructive habits
- Taking control over your own emotional well-being
- Discovering the real obstacles standing between you and the things you want in life
- Forgiving yourself for past mistakes and bad experiences while turning them into positive learning experiences
- Replacing the roller coaster of success and failure with consistent results
- Letting the small stuff slide without beating yourself up over it

- Replacing your negative addictions with positive addictions that will transform your life into an exciting adventure that just keeps getting better and better

So... how do you go about doing this?

Breaking the Spell

Breaking the spell of your own hypnosis begins with clarity about what you really want in your life. The next step is to accept full responsibility for your feelings. You need not be responsible for how you feel or what caused those feelings. You need only be responsible for changing how you feel when needed. Responsibility for changing your feelings is the very first step of letting go and freeing yourself to grow into resourceful instincts and productive patterns.

Not taking responsibility for how you feel helps you avoid falling into the trap of self-judging. Remember that the path to letting go is paved with freedom from guilt, self-acceptance, and self-love. Your non-resourceful beliefs, emotions, feelings, and actions brought you to this point of being able to make conscious choices. You would not be the person you are today without all aspects of yourself, including the non-resourceful aspects.

The desire to change your circumstances is fine but will not actually do anything by itself. You must make the conscious decision to change the rules you live by and then act on that decision. Anything less is wishful thinking such as trying to use the Law of Attraction. It won't work.

Achieving a different result in your life requires you to take different action. Taking different action requires you to know something different to do. Knowing something different to do requires you to at least suspect that happiness cannot be where you have been looking or you would have already found it. You must be open to trying a new way and to changing the rules of your game.

This is the only way to change your life. This is the only way to alter the waveform to make things that seem impossible into real possibilities and even likelihoods. This is the only way to make real whatever it is you want. This is putting the Law of Realization to conscious use instead of letting it happen on autopilot.

Saying this is easy. Making the decision is easy. Embarking on your new path is easy. Staying on this path long enough to make real lasting changes is the challenge because of your current emotional addictions that form your comfort zone. Your initial feelings of joy and progress will soon give in to a growing list of excuses why you cannot and must not proceed. This is your survival instincts telling you to get back in your comfort zone before some predator kills and eats you. This is perfectly normal. It means your prey brain is working as it should.

The key is to keep going no matter what. We will talk about this more in Chapter 16. Eventually the whispers in your head urging you to stop will begin urging you to keep going. That will be your first indication that you are becoming addicted to positive emotions, feelings, and beliefs by reprogramming your brain.

Be Fully Present

The best way to break any addiction is to live in the moment by being fully present during every moment. Being fully present is the path to happiness because happiness is as easy as living in each moment with no attachment.

Everything you accomplished in your life happened when you lived in the moment. Many people think they are living in the moment when all they are doing is running from one moment to the next. Be here now! Nothing else matters. If something bad happens, let yourself feel it. Let it pass through you. Don't look back once it's gone. Do the same thing when something good happens. It's all neutral anyway. Good and bad only exist inside your head.

Your life is happening at every single moment. Why not be an active part of it instead of losing the present by focusing on past or future? Being actively present in every moment means connecting with your senses and observing what is happening inside and around you. It means paying attention to your thoughts, feelings, and actions.

We often hear that happiness comes from within. This much is true because happiness does not and cannot exist anywhere but within you. We rarely hear what this truth means and a message that should be liberating can be misleading. It can even be a trap because we can conclude that happiness comes from a non-material source such as God or some guru, leader, or spiritual teacher. This misperception has far too many people chasing happiness without ever really finding it.

Happiness does come from within because the universe is a completely neutral place. Good and bad do not exist unless and until you label something good or bad. Imagine a plate of seafood. The dish itself is just seafood and there is nothing good or bad about it. Jim loves seafood. He labels the dish good. Anthony dislikes seafood. He labels the dish bad. The dish itself remains exactly the same either way.

A decision made now creates a result now. Hanging onto a decision changes future decisions. How has hanging on worked out for you? Forget logic and reason. Humans are emotional animals. Use your instincts. Embrace your intuition. Drink in your senses. See happiness. Hear happiness. Feel happiness. Smell happiness. Taste happiness. Be in your happiness and you will find happiness.

This is not the plastered-on smile and wishful thinking that comes with the Law of Attraction. This is taking action to always observe yourself and choose how to respond at every moment of every day. Plan for the future, let go of the past, and live in the moment where the action is and where happiness and love are always present. We will talk about this more in Chapter 16.

The Key to Success

Ignorance is one of the leading causes of unhappiness and limited success because we tend to ignore what we really want and focus on our worries. The keys to getting what you want in life are:

- Clarity about what you want
- Taking action to change
- Self observation to see things as they happen and make conscious choices about how to respond
- Letting go of everything that does not support what you want

Focusing on each moment lets you make your moments better. Making better moments improves what comes later. Being clear about what you want allows you to choose how to respond to life events. Your responses change the range of possible outcomes because they alter the waveform. You already respond to everything that happens. Why not respond consciously instead of automatically?

You can consciously choose your feelings or let yourself drift in a sea of emotions. Events, actions, and results can't product happiness on their own. Treat them with indifference. Remember that there is no such thing as good or bad until you apply those labels. The key is to apply those labels consciously.

A person's capacity for emotions is like a bucket that only holds so much liquid. Choosing to see things as bad reduces your capacity for accomplishing what you want. The reverse is also true. Hanging on to past hurts keeps emotional liquid in your buckets and limits your ability to take on more. A bucket full of emotional waste is like the filthy furniture factory we discussed in Chapter 9 that keeps you from living your true potential by limiting your ability to give and receive love, happiness, and connect with your true inner power.

Each moment is a new opportunity for freedom. You can learn to avoid blind reactions to emotional triggers and to create an observer inside yourself who alerts you to events and reminds you to choose joy and to see the bright side of everything. You don't need to master or get over your bad feelings. Just empty the bucket.

Try a simple exercise: Stop what you are doing and go take a walk for fifteen minutes. During your walk, focus all of your attention on experiencing each moment and see what happens. Do this every day and the results will surprise you. Learn to do this during every waking moment and the results will astound you. You will learn that the destinations you imagine in your mind mean nothing because the journey is what matters.

Accept what comes without question and without resistance. You can't change what comes at you in life. You can choose how you interpret and respond to each thing that comes along. You don't need any kind of special system or guru to show you the way. All you need to do is live life on your own terms.

You are already doing that anyway. If you don't like what you have created then simply change the terms you live by. All you have to do is keep telling yourself what those terms are moment by moment. This requires both losing your attachments and engaging in conscious self observation.

The *Cracking the Life Code* series by Jim walks you through the process of identifying and letting go of negative emotions, feelings, thoughts, and beliefs.

The Enlightened Savage and *The Natural Savage* by Anthony Hernandez delve into the human prey brain and explore the evolutionary roots of everything we do every day.

* * *

Chapter 14: Lose Your Attachments

There is a great story of some fishermen in one of the old countries who sailed before dawn to fish until mid afternoon. They returned to unload their catch on the dock and spend the rest of the afternoon preparing for the next day of fishing. Their wives used this time to load the catch in baskets and go to market.

One day they had to go to a market that was farther away and would require an overnight stay. The women began looking for a good spot to bed down as darkness fell. One woman suggested sleeping in a beautiful meadow full of wild flowers. They set their fish baskets at the edge of the meadow and walked out into the flowers with their lovely smell and lay down to sleep. They tossed and turned for hours but sleep would not come. Finally one of the women picked up her blanket, walked to the edge of the meadow where the smelly baskets of fish were, lay down, and went right to sleep.

The moral of the story is that we can get so attached to our own stinking circumstances and old beliefs that we close ourselves off to any other way of doing things. We hypnotize ourselves with our own inner dialogue. We create this image of a lovely meadow with sweet-smelling flowers only to surrender to the belief that we need the familiar stench of fish to be comfortable. This is the survival instinct telling us to get back into our comfort zone before some predator kills and eats us.

Nothing is Permanent

Everything changes. You cannot un-spill a cup of coffee. Bodies age and eventually die. There are no guarantees in life. Anything and everything in our lives that we are not directly observing right now could have changed. The only guarantee we have is that nothing in our lives is permanent. We ourselves are not permanent.

Everything that we think of as good in our lives will vanish at some point. The same is true for everything we think of as bad. It's a zero-sum game because there is no such thing as intrinsic good or bad.

Attaching or identifying yourself with anything in your life by saying, "I am ____" is therefore a recipe for eventual disaster. A friend of Anthony's whose wife committed suicide spent a year "finding a new normal" because he identified a huge part of himself as, "I am a husband." Losing his wife caused him to lose a huge part of his identity. This was an incredibly traumatic experience.

Realizing the impermanence of everything is incredibly liberating. Everything in life is like a piece of cake that you are eating. You know full well that the cake will eventually be finished and yet you free yourself to enjoy it while it lasts without any grief or regret or "finding yourself" once the plate is empty. The ironic part is that the cake ends up being far more "you" than most things in your life because its atoms and molecules become part of your body.

Expect Nothing

Being unattached removes all expectations. Expectations are a zero-sum game at best. If you give something to somebody and expect something back from that person then the best you can do is break even. You lose if the other person does not meet your expectations.

Give something to somebody freely without any expectations and the worst you can do is break even. Same for the other person. Removing all expectations creates a no-lose proposition for everyone. Loving someone with no attachments lets you love them freely in the moment. Loving someone without expectations means that everything you receive from that person will be a gift. That special someone can include yourself.

You have very little control over the many events and people in your life. This means that you have very little real power to meet your need for control. It's OK to want things and to plan and move toward goals. It's OK to want love and meaningful relationships. Just don't attach yourself to any particular outcome and don't expect anything in particular to happen. If letting go of negative emotions puts out a burning fire then non-attachment prevents the fire from igniting in the first place.

Nothing is Good or Bad

There is a Chinese proverb about a farmer who had a prize stallion. One day the stallion escaped and ran off. His neighbors offered their condolences for this misfortune but the farmer replied, "Good or bad? Who knows?" The stallion returned three days later leading a herd of wild horses. The neighbors congratulated the farmer on his good fortune but he replied, "Good or bad, who knows?" The farmer's son tried to ride one of the horses but fell off and broke his leg. Again the neighbors offered their condolences and again the farmer replied, "Good or bad, who knows?" The army came through several days later to conscript able-bodied men to go off and fight. The farmer's son was exempted because of his injury. So it went.

So it goes in all of our lives. The only question is whether or not we can remain unattached enough to see the neutrality and opportunity in everything that can possibly happen to us. Non-attachment is an expression of control. You constantly remind yourself not to attach yourself, which means you exercise control over your identity and your emotions.

Life and everything about it is completely and totally neutral unless and until we choose to apply a label to it. We make these choices all the time but only rarely do so consciously.

Peace is Powerful

It is very easy to get upset and make threats or even pick a fight. It is much more difficult to remain peaceful. Peace is especially hard when someone is trying to get you riled up or when someone is wronging you in some way. You will discover that the need for peace is greatest when you most want to be anything but peaceful.

This does not mean that you need to let people walk all over you. This is not what letting go is about. Simply letting others have their way with you and avoiding all conflict is not peaceful. It is in fact violent because you are letting yourself be abused. Be a wall. A wall is solid. It lets nothing past. Your need for control remains on one side. The hurts and abuses from others remain on the other side.

If you need something then state what you need. If there is a situation you cannot accept then don't accept it. Just be peaceful about it. Your wall has enough gates in it to let things in and out as needed. You can be flexible when you need to be.

Clinging to the need for control such as making threats and ultimatums and bossing others around only makes it less likely that you will get your way. Demonstrating peace and good faith and unconditional respect by letting go of your need to control things and people makes it more likely that you will get your way.

Self observation and letting go of the need for control is nothing more than accepting that life is simply life and that different types of people are just a part of life. Sometimes you find people and things that you choose to call good. Sometimes you will get things that you choose to label as good, and sometimes bad. Only when you understand and accept this can you truly be free.

Chapter 15: Observe Yourself

All emotions involve energy. The word *emotion* breaks down to "energy in motion." Increasing the energy of a photon causes its frequency to rise from the radio and microwave bands at the low end of the spectrum through the infrared, visible light, ultraviolet, X-ray, and gamma bands.

Hopeless people are like a photon at the lowest end of the spectrum. People who are at peace are like photons at the highest ends of that same spectrum. The brighter the light, the more photons are traveling. The stronger the emotion, the stronger the underlying beliefs. Photons color everything we see. Our beliefs color everything we perceive with emotion. Our beliefs emit the "photons" of emotion.

Emotions are our responses to the things that happen in our lives. The things themselves are never good nor bad. They just are. Negative core beliefs project a low-frequency emotion that will move you farther away from your true self and drains your resources. Letting go of a non-resourceful emotion literally frees up the energy that is being spent on that emotion for you to use for something more productive. Why not direct that liberated energy toward a positive outcome for your life?

This has nothing to do with thinking positive or putting on a happy face. This has nothing to do with affirmations, even though affirmations can help you prepare for the "moment of truth" when you experience an emotion or (even better) recognize an event and choose how to label it. This has everything to do with releasing the energy that is generated by, and that reinforces, your negative beliefs.

Letting go of negative emotions before they take hold is crucial in the same way that putting out a fire before it spreads is crucial. Letting go must happen in the present. You can't go back in time to un-light a fire or skip ahead to put it out in the future. Letting go frees you from the pain of the past or the worries about the future. Now is where the action is and where the solution is. Letting go comes from a place of loving yourself.

The best way to put out a fire is to prevent it from happening in the first place. The best way to let go of a negative emotion is to never experience that emotion in the first place. Experiencing a negative emotion alerts you to something that you need to let go of. This requires you to realize some very fundamental truths and develop the art of non-attachment that we talked about in Chapter 14. It also requires keen self observation to expose the core beliefs that have remained hidden in plain view your entire life. this is not attraction or manifestation; it is self observation.

The negative emotion is the energy of that core belief surfacing to protect you from being killed and eaten. The negative emotion is your friend, not your enemy. When it comes up embrace it, observe it, and then allow it to leave peacefully and with your heartfelt thanks for a job well done but no longer needed.

Conscious Choice

Your emotions are both the cause and the result of your thoughts and actions. Most of us don't consciously choose how to interpret the events in our lives. This means that you have already labeled them as good or bad by the time you experience the emotion. The emotion is already positive or negative by the time you feel it and is either drawing you closer to or further away from where you want to go.

Letting go means recognizing the emotion when you experience it and choosing to stop having that emotion. This happens when your logic kicks in to rationalize or explain the emotion. Letting go of the emotion means that you only experience it for a few seconds (at best) or that its intensity and/or duration is reduced. This is a good thing!

Letting go of your attachments and expectations helps prevent negative emotions from happening in the first place. This is ultimately where you want to be. This requires conscious self observation to accomplish.

The other aspect of conscious choice involves living your life on purpose. How many choices do you make by default every day? If you are in a relationship then you continue on in that relationship. If you have a job then you keep going to work every day. You go about your routine because it is routine. This is how most people live their lives because humans are prey animals that depend on routines.

On the other hand, imagine making new choices every day. Imagine waking up every morning and choosing to really be with your significant other. How would making this choice influence your behavior toward that person or how you interpret their behavior?

The word *responsibility* breaks down as "ability to respond." Having the ability to respond means that you have a choice. Choice is power. Making a conscious choice gives you full responsibility for everything that choice involves. Giving yourself the freedom to choose gives you the ability to respond to life in the moment.

For example, choosing to be with your significant other every morning for just that one day gives you the freedom to leave whenever you like. The freedom to leave gives you the freedom to stay. This freedom in turn gives you the freedom to truly be with your significant other. Every time you think about or interact with your significant other gives you the opportunity to select the response from the available options that best honors your decision to be with that person. This is an extremely powerful example of how conscious choice and self observation can alter a waveform to make real a better relationship!

Getting to the point where you start automatically making conscious choices requires careful and ongoing self observation. This develops the ability to make conscious decisions whenever something happens. It's like having a little person on your shoulder who alerts you whenever something happens and lets you make a conscious decision about how to interpret that inherently neutral event. We call this little person on your shoulder the *conscious interrupt*.

Good Intentions Are Not Enough

Intention is where change begins. Just having the intention is enough to start skewing the waveform and the range of possible circumstances toward the desired outcome. Self-knowledge is where wisdom and transformation begin. Nobody can give this to you. Every person must find this for herself or himself. Far too many people think they can change themselves by changing their circumstances, the people around them, their jobs, etc. This is inaccurate because we need to know ourselves first in order to know what to change.

Transformation itself begins with fully understanding exactly where you are and how you got to this point. The truth may hurt but it will also set you free. You and you alone know your own truth. No self-help expert can give this to you.

There is no magic bullet nor is there some correct path to your truth. The only way to find your truth is to observe yourself. Intention starts a process that only self observation can continue. Self observation simply means to seek self-knowledge before taking action. Self observation asks, "Is this taking me in the direction I want to go?" at every opportunity. Stop asking what you should be doing until you know what you need to understand.

Self observation is the act of being consciously aware of what you are thinking, feeling, saying, and doing. For example, if you feel afraid then you can step back and see the reasons for that fear. This opens the door to understanding that fear is nothing more than recurring thoughts and feelings about situations that may or may not even be real.

The feelings you have can be about how you think life should be, how others should be, past events, future events, or how you can manipulate or try to control people and situations to get what you want. None of these feelings have anything at all to do with the present and yet the present is the only moment that is real.

Using the Conscious Interrupt

Your beliefs set up cycles of emotional addiction that nature designed to keep you from being killed and eaten. Simply replacing your beliefs is not enough because that old data remains in your brain and could creep back into use. More on this in a moment. Meanwhile, the only way to permanently overwrite your old beliefs is through self observation and the conscious interrupt.

The conscious interrupt is exactly what the name implies. It interrupts old patterns and beliefs. You are consciously aware of it at all times. This is the little person sitting on your shoulder watching your life like a hawk. This little person is always vigilant and never sleeps. He interrupts you every time something happens like a ringing telephone that disturbs your thoughts. This reminds you that you have a choice to make about how to interpret the event that just happened or is about to happen and whether it is leading you down the correct path.

The whole idea is to replace the choices you already make unconsciously with similar choices that you can make consciously. This is what allows you to begin using the Law of Realization consciously instead of unconsciously. Conscious decisions are the only thing that will break your old negative addiction and replace it with a more positive addiction.

Making conscious decisions will become your new survival routine that you will stick to just as fiercely as the survival routines you have been clinging to. This is what we mean when we say that you can use your prey brain and hard-wired survival instincts to your advantage.

Begin Observing Yourself Today

Start observing every thought, feeling, emotion, word, and action. Think of it like having that little person on your shoulder watching everything coming to and from you. Every word and action comes from your feelings and beliefs. Transformation happens when you let go of the emotions that hold the underlying belief in place.

Letting go is not as difficult as some believe. You actually let go just by observing the negative emotion, choosing not to react by making the wrong choice, and using the opportunity to make a different choice that takes you in the direction you want to go.

We have seen how the human prey brain works and how our core beliefs affect our entire lives. You know that nothing that happens is ever intrinsically good or bad unless and until you choose how to interpret and label it. You also know that you are always labeling your experiences either consciously or unconsciously.

There are plenty of systems that claim to remove old limiting beliefs or reprogram your brain. These systems may or may not work but even the best system cannot guarantee success. Deleting something from a computer does not remove that data. All the information remains on your hard drive and slowly gets buried under new information over days, months, or even years.

You can buy programs that undelete erased data. There are even programs that can look at every scrap of old data on that hard drive. Your brain contains a powerful undelete feature. This is great for preserving and recalling memories but comes with potential negative side effects. For example, you will find your old programming creeping back into use unless you actively keep knocking it back like a stubborn weed. This requires continuous self-examination.

Develop the habit of observing yourself at every moment of every day. Whenever you feel a non-resourceful feeling, observe yourself having the feeling and ask where it comes from. Don't worry if you can't identify the source for all feelings. Ask yourself if this feeling is real or related to some past experience. The habit of asking is more important than having answers all the time.

If you can't identify where the feeling originated, simply let go of the feeling you have right now. For example, if you are feeling frustration and can't identify where it originated then just let go of the frustration.

If you want to take this experience to a whole different level, try asking yourself, "Is this frustration coming from my need to control?" If so, then let go of the need to control the outcome. Doing this disconnects you from all of the feelings that come from the need to control.

Observe your every action during the day as if you were watching someone else. Hear every word and the tone of your voice. See your gestures, actions, thoughts, and feelings. Be aware of your beliefs filtering everything you perceive. Maintain this intense level of observation all day.

Here are some common thoughts and feelings that people often have and some suggested ways to use those times for self observation and letting go:

- Instead of asking, "Why does this always happen to me?" ask yourself, "What feeling am I holding inside that creates or facilitates this painful situation?"
- Instead of thinking, "I am worried about my future." ask yourself, "Can the worry I'm feeling help me find a solution to my problem?"
- Instead of wondering, "Why is this person acting the way they are?" ask yourself, "What part of me wants to suffer over how this person is acting?"
- Instead of demanding, "Why are people always taking advantage of me?" ask yourself, "Who is this 'me' that always wants to be the victim?"
- Instead of worrying about, "Have I made the right decision?" ask yourself, "What feeling inside of me is causing me to be fearf
- ul?"
- Instead of wanting to know, "Why doesn't this person see how wrong they are?" ask yourself, "Is my need to control that person good for either of us?"

Don't let any part of you go unobserved. You will soon start to understand that many of your daily actions have little value beyond attempting to get you more approval or control.

Keep up the daily observation. It will be tough at first but does get easier over time and will eventually become second-nature. Consistent self observation and letting go will eventually begin to change your current addictive programming. You will start to see opportunities to take more appropriate actions towards your short-and long-term goals. This will alter the waveform in your favor while creating positive addictions at the same time.

Develop Your Skills

Results will be small at first and will grow over time. You will start by catching yourself after the fact when it's too late. Don't beat yourself up for not catching yourself! Instead, be glad and thankful that you did catch yourself as you ask yourself why you did what you did.

Keep doing this and you will begin catching yourself in mid-action. This is great progress! Be happy for your progress and ask yourself why you are in the middle of doing whatever you are doing.

Don't stop there. Your self observation skills will eventually reach the point where you catch yourself before acting. This gives you the opportunity to ask yourself which action is the most appropriate to getting what you want. Here is a hint: The most correct action is usually the most peaceful action possible.

* * *

Chapter 16: The Six Ingredients of Letting Go

Making any sort of change in your life requires six ingredients. Using only five ingredients may work but you will have a much harder time of it. Cutting back to four will make your efforts all but futile. The ingredients themselves are simple. Using the ingredients is simple in theory. In practice, these ingredients are the foundation of the "rehab" you need to go through to break your current negative addictions and replace them with more positive ones.

Actually using the ingredients will therefore become harder and harder as your prey brain fights desperately to cling to its survival programming and keep you from getting killed and eaten. You must therefore proceed forward with utter determination following the process we will discuss in Chapter 19. You must do this from a place of never judging or punishing yourself for any past failings or for succumbing to any of the obstacles you will throw in your own path.

The resistance you will feel is perfectly natural. It means that your survival instincts are working as they should. It is important to love and honor these old instincts and to be gentle with yourself at all times. Withdrawing from any addiction is a tough process but it will get better. The old saying about the sky being darkest just before the dawn holds true here.

You will see a positive result each time you consciously let go but will often meet with emotional conflict. This is your old survival programming trying to get you to keep hanging on. Don't listen! Remember that the old programs are not hanging onto you. You are hanging onto them. You are in control here. It's your choice whether to push "Delete" or "Enter."

There is another interesting fact about the dawning of a new day that you should be aware of. The coldest part of the day does not come just before the sun rises. This moment actually happens some time after daybreak because the amount of solar energy is not yet high enough to stop the cooling. Solar energy increases as the sun rises until it eventually becomes strong enough to stop the cooling and begin the daily warming.

What this means for you is that the process of letting go will keep getting harder. You will eventually begin to see the light at the end of the tunnel and may start to feel like you are so close but yet so far. This is your best indication that you are almost at the end of your old programming… which is also near the beginning of your new programming. This is a signal to keep going!

What are the six ingredients?

Desire to Change

This ingredient is so obvious that including it may seem silly. You have to have the desire to change in order to make those changes. Nothing and nobody can force you to do this. The choice is always yours no matter what situation you may be in.

The desire to change alone starts to tip the waveform and make what you want more possible but you cannot stop there. Remember what we said in Chapter 3: The Law of Attraction is real. You can make something appear just by wanting it but the odds are so low that you shouldn't even try. The Law of Attraction fails as a practical tool because it relies on this one ingredient alone.

The Law of Realization works all day every day whether you want it to or not and whether you are aware of it or not. Putting the Law of Realization to conscious use requires the five remaining ingredients.

Have a Clear Intention

You must make a firm decision about just what you want in your life. Make this decision in a way that does not allow for anything less. Allowing yourself to settle for something less creates wiggle room that your prey survival instincts will exploit to the fullest to keep you in your current comfort zone. Figure out exactly what you want and then keep your eyes on the prize with laser-like focus.

Making the decision to change creates raw intention that will direct you to focus your attention on what you want. Knowing exactly what you want focuses your attention on that exact spot. Intention creates attention. Without intention you won't know what to focus your attention upon. Not knowing exactly what you want blurs and scatters your attention.

You now have made the decision to change and know exactly what those changes look like. Here is where things start to get interesting.

Be Bold

You have to be bold! Look around you. At least ninety five percent of the people in the world are stuck not living the lives they want. Follow their example and you will end up just like them. Step away from the crowd. Everyone is an example for others. Most examples are warnings about what not to do. A very few examples guide us toward what we should do. Be a positive example.

Society is just one aspect of boldness. Facing the fact that you are a junkie addicted to negative emotional patterns is the other.

Going into rehab is an incredibly tough and brave thing to do but it will not work without sheer boldness.

Be Uncomfortable

Look back on your life and you can probably recite a long litany of failures, people who have hurt you, people you have hurt, and the many other skeletons lurking in your mental closet. Everyone has a list like this that may include our parents, schoolteachers, spouses, children, best friends, business partners, and more. These old pains lead to avoidance in the same way that you instantly pull your hand back if you accidentally touch a hot surface.

Avoiding one hot surface causes us to avoid other hot surfaces. This is a good thing if we are talking about hot stoves but can become a problem when we are talking about emotions. Avoiding emotional hurts can cause us to develop prejudiced thinking and perceptions that drive us to withdraw and avoid other people or act in other negative ways. This is natural because we are prey animals.

We begin to judge and fear others. We judge ourselves. We fear change. We form opinions about anyone or anything that we fear might cause us any sort of pain. Most of us spend our whole lives attempting to avoid discomfort at all cost. We see ourselves as victims and do all we can to take control over our whole lives. We saw in Chapter 12 that this obsessive need for control actually causes us to be out of control.

Meanwhile, our lives are passing us by while we waste precious time and life energy defending our false beliefs, and yet defending those false beliefs is what most of us define as our "comfort zone!"

You must be willing to leave your old comfort zone way behind you. Letting go can sometimes be uncomfortable. Facing your fears and doing something in a different way than you have done in the past requires a level of discomfort. Discomfort is good because it proves that you are making progress. If you are comfortable then you are not making progress. It is that simple.

You must challenge the survival programming in your brain that is keeping you stuck in your current patterns and this is a very uncomfortable thing to do. Remember that your brain interprets leaving the comfort zone as risking you being killed and eaten. Your brain wants to keep you alive and will do all it can to shove you back inside that comfort zone.

Let Go

You have to learn to let go. Letting go of your fundamental need to control everything liberates you from all sorts of negative emotional patterns such as the examples in Chapter 11. Losing the need for control does not mean losing control. All it means is that you are giving up trying to mold your world, the people in your life, and your circumstances however you want them to be.

Letting go gives you the room to create a sense of peace, joy, and flow in your life that you cannot create any other way. Think about the happiest times in your life and you will soon see that all of them occurred when you were in the moment and going along with the flow.

Letting go of an unwanted emotion, feeling, behavior, or belief frees up mental space to accept and make real whatever it is you do want just like deleting a file on a hard drive leaves more room for new files. Stop focusing on what you don't want. It has not worked for you and will never work for you.

For example, focusing on a bad prior relationship will blind you from seeing Mrs. or Mr. Right when she or he does show up. Any new relationship you do go into will begin with the bitter taste of the old relationship. We think you would agree that this is hardly an auspicious beginning.

If you want to have a loving relationship or anything else in the present then you have to take off the rose-colored glasses from the past.

Realize

Desire, decision, boldness, discomfort, and letting go are great but they cannot work unless and until you take the correct action. Try this simple experiment sometime: Get in your car, sit down, buckle up, and then think about starting the engine. Don't be surprised when nothing happens. Try yelling and screaming at your car to start. Pound the steering wheel if you like.

These are all actions but none of them is the correct action because your car will refuse to start. Now put the key in the ignition and turn it. Notice that the car starts right up. The next step after starting the engine is to consciously drive the car.

Clear intention creates live energy and inaction drains that energy. Using that energy correctly equals action. Misusing that energy creates needless stress. We all need times of peaceful thought and non-action from time to time but these times are usually way less valuable than ideas backed up by correct action.

Think result. This is always the first step in achieving that result. The next step is to actively create that result. Combining your intention with correct action while letting go of anything that does not lead you toward your intended result will tip the waveform in the right direction. This is you consciously putting the Law of Realization to work instead of simply letting things happen to you.

Tipping the waveform in the right direction improves the odds of you getting the results you seek from practically impossible to possible, likely, and very likely. There are never any guarantees but if you keep tipping the odds far enough in your favor then you are almost bound to see good results at some point.

Never forget that nothing can ever happen without action. Thinking good thoughts, wishing for what you want, writing down your goals, pumping yourself full of motivation, and plastering on a happy and grateful smile no matter what will not do anything but create even more stuff that you'll have to deal with and let go of later on.

If you want something then make it real. It is that simple. Doing this may require a lot or work but should require zero struggle. We will explain this in the next chapter. The process of making something real consists of the four steps that you will see in Chapter 19.

Don't stop there. Your self observation skills will eventually reach the point where you catch yourself before acting. This gives you the opportunity to ask yourself which action is the most appropriate to getting what you want.

The hint at the end of Chapter 15 bears repeating: The most correct action is usually the most peaceful action possible.

For step-by-step help with letting go, please pick up one or more titles from the *Cracking the Life Code* series by Jim. You will also enjoy *The Enlightened Savage* and *The Natural Savage* by Anthony Hernandez.

* * *

Chapter 17: Redefining Work

Imagine the example of two identical piles of dirt that must each be moved an identical distance. Person A tackles the job using a tiny toy shovel and bucket. It takes him days of backbreaking work to complete the job. Person B uses a tractor to move the entire pile in less than a minute.

Person A was at it for days. Person B was there for one minute. Who did more work? Most people we ask say that Person A did more work. A few say that Person B did more work.

The Real Meaning of Work

Both answers are wrong. Person A and Person B did exactly the same amount of work. The people who select Person A tend to confuse "work" with "struggle." This means that they confuse the end result with the effort required to obtain that result. The people who select Person B tend to confuse "work" with "time."

Physics defines *work* as output. Work is therefore not a measure of effort but of results. The only difference in this example is that Person A struggled to achieve what Person B did with ease. If you relate "success" with "hard work" then chances are that you are wasting a good part of your life struggling for no good reason. If you equate "success" with "ease" then you will get results with the least possible effort.

This simple fact explains why most of us never achieve the success we seek. Society teaches us to define "work" as "struggle." Everyone is expected to go to school for more than twenty years so that they can spend the next forty years struggling to save up enough money to get in a few rounds of golf before leaving this world. That is slavery!

Self-employed people are no different. Any business that depends on its owners for survival has slaves for owners. This kind of slavery is even worse because anyone can quit and find a new job but closing a business is far more difficult. Business owners have the advantage of being able to design their businesses to not require them but few of them ever do.

Most people resign themselves to slavery and blame anyone and anything but themselves for their problems because they insist on defining work as effort instead of results. There is no such thing as luck. There are people who always look for ways to make getting what they want easier and there are people who don't.

Everybody has the exact same potential for success and the exact same chance to achieve everything they want in life. The difference between those who achieve the success they seek and those who don't boils down to core beliefs. If your core beliefs and survival instincts are not serving you then it's high time to change them so that you can reshape the waveform to your advantage.

The Cycle Continues

Society places expectations on us and we do our best to live up to them to gain acceptance. This creates a cycle of emotional addiction that keeps us in the rat race. Some people dare to think outside the box by purchasing self-help materials or switching careers. What usually ends up happening is that they interpret all of the self-help programs, books, tapes, etc. to validate their current beliefs instead of suggesting new ones to adopt.

What did the people around you teach you about success? What did you learn from your parents, teachers, friends, clergy, associates, bosses, the media, etc. about money, happiness, wealth, and success? How did your parents and others around you view work, struggle, success, money, and fulfillment? Were you told that rich people are greedy crooks or that you can't have everything you want?

How do the people closest to you live their lives and what are the results? What specific life experiences affected your beliefs? When were these beliefs formed? It may surprise you to know that most of your beliefs were in place by age two.

Here is the truth:

- You will struggle if you believe that success requires struggle.
- You will never be rich if you think that rich people are greedy criminals.
- You will remain poor if you believe that money is the root of all evil.
- This same logic applies to emotions, thoughts, and everything else in each of our lives.

What if today you saw some of the things you saw as a child for the very first time? It is a safe bet that you would react quite differently than you did back then. Adults know they can interpret what they see, hear, feel, taste, and smell. For example, two people on the same tropical vacation may interpret the same events in very different ways.

* * *

Chapter 18: You Can Do It

Your brain will do everything it can think of to keep you in your current cycle because your whole body is addicted to that cycle and the emotional cocktails it produces. Any deviation from this tells your brain that your chances of being killed and eaten are much higher. Your brain will resist change even when that change is beneficial and healthy.

Anthony had a coaching client who wanted to start a business. The client's parents and friends advised her against it because "it's too hard." I asked her some very simple questions: Who are these people? Are they rich? Are they living the lives they want or are they struggling? You can guess the answers to all of these questions!

The lesson is clear: If you need a teacher then find someone who is doing what it is you want to do. If you want to be rich, learn from a rich person. If you want to learn sales, learn from the best salesman you can find. Make it a point to always learn from people whose beliefs challenge your own. This forces your mind to open up and absorb more information.

Master Each Step

Imagine casting your old beliefs aside and are just waiting for the good stuff to rain down on you. You wait and wait but nothing happens. The universe obeys quantum laws that guarantee you will never simply manifest your dreams by thinking happy thought. The intention to change tips the waveform. That is a crucial first step. If this was the only step then the Law of Attraction would function exactly as advertised. Intention is great for motivation but not so much for actual building.

Pretend you have a toddler who is accustomed to drinking water from plastic kiddy cups. One evening he asks you to pour his water into a grown up cup. You grant his request by handing him a plastic cup with no lid. The toddler goes to take a sip and drops the glass. Water splashes all over the place.

You would probably grab some paper towels and mop up the mess without too much protest. Everyone makes mistakes. No big deal. Now imagine coming back with a fresh glass of water to see Junior reaching for an adult cup made of glass. You would probably snatch the glass from his hand.

Junior proved he cannot handle a small plastic cup. There is no way he can manage a bigger cup made of glass. You also don't want to set him up for failure by giving him more than he can handle. Breaking a glass can also cause nasty cuts. Keeping Junior within safe limits is extremely important.

If you have not mastered your current life and situation then you can never find lasting satisfaction. There is a slim possibility that you could handle more but that is not the way to bet. Mastering your life as it exists today through letting go and self observation shifts your waveform enough to let you try bigger projects and roles on for size.

There are no shortcuts. If you do not have the life of your dreams then chances are excellent you have not yet learned to master your current life. For example, if you seek wealth but cannot handle one hundred dollars then you cannot manage one million. You must always start where you are no matter what.

Learn to manage what you have. Live within your means. Know where your money is coming from and where it is going. Account for every cent. Begin saving some of your money. You may be in a tight or even dire situation. That is OK. Learning to manage what you have is the shortest and easiest escape from your situation. This same logic holds for anything in your life.

You Are Priceless

Take a moment to consider just how small the odds were of you being born. One tiny slip-up in your lineage millions or even billions of years ago and you would not be here to read this book in your current form. Just by being alive you are incredibly lucky.

The universe has existed for about 13.7 billion years. At no point during this time has there ever been a being just like you. You will never be replaced in your current form after your time here is over.

Humans value things by how rare they are. Each of us is one of a kind. Each of us is therefore a priceless jewel. If that knowledge doesn't inspire you then we don't know what will. Anything less than living to your potential is literally an event of cosmic proportions.

Breaking Through

Everyone has doubts, fears, and insecurity no matter how much money they have or how happy they are in life. This is normal. These non-resourceful feelings are like a mountain looming in your path. You can choose to walk miles out of your way to try to get over or around this mountain. You can also decide to take a shortcut and tunnel straight through the mountain.

Breaking through by letting go of emotional baggage, engaging in keen self observation, and developing a robust conscious interrupt is the best way to make positive changes in your life. This method focuses on your strengths and what is right with you instead of focusing on what's wrong and trying to apply patches and fixes. We believe that most if not all of your challenges exist because your brain is working perfectly to execute its programming.

There are psychological and psychiatric disorders that require intervention by properly trained and certified mental health practitioners. We are not doctors and cannot give any medical advice. What we can do is ask you to take a serious look at the possibility that you are far more OK than you think you are.

Let go of your emotional baggage. You don't need it. All it's doing is weighing you down. Concentrate on the idea that you are a priceless and unique human being. You deserve every success!

Chapter 19: The Process of Making Real

We learned in Chapter 16 that the sixth ingredient of letting go is taking correct action to make what you want real. You already know that taking this action will challenge your survival programming and put you into a state of withdrawal from your old emotional addictions. This easy four-step process helps you make gradual changes and ease the struggle of that withdrawal. The four steps are:

- **Step One: Define your goal.** What would you like to accomplish during the next few short weeks? Think about this in terms of beginning a long journey that you will take on foot. Be absolutely clear about your intentions and destination.

- **Step Two: Pick easy milestones.** Set off from your starting location with your end goal in mind and you will be hot, tired, sweaty, and ready to call the whole thing off within minutes. Forget the destination. Life is a journey. You are not at your destination. Worrying about it is pointless. Take small steps and look at your feet. Celebrate every step for the real and measurable progress that it represents.

  Like a loaded freight train at rest, you will need some time to get up to speed. Slow gentle acceleration is the best way to ramp up.

  Like a loaded freight train barreling down the tracks, you'll have lots of momentum and won't want to stop once you hit your stride. Be bold!

- **Step Three: Perform the task.** You must actually take the step when the time is right. Action is key. Don't sit around daydreaming about what you want. Don't try to attract or manifest anything unless you have many billions or even trillions of years to spare.

  Where you have been and where you are going don't matter at all. Just look at your feet and celebrate each step as you take it. Set a clear destination for the step that you can see and accomplish with as much ease as possible. Define criteria for success and give yourself a deadline. Then do it.

- **Step Four: Reward yourself.** This in many ways is the most important step. We are so used to beating ourselves up for doing wrong that we forget how much better it is to reward ourselves for doing right. Make this a habit. You'll like it.

Define a reward for each step of each journey you take. You get the reward if you accomplish your step on time according to the success criteria you defined. You do not get the reward if you do not accomplish the step. Never punish yourself. Just don't reward yourself for falling short.

Punishment can never be an option. We have all had quite enough pain in our lives. Pain is probably what drove you to pick up this book in the first place.

Every reward you give yourself must be original in the sense that it must be both creative and something you don't usually do or have. It must also be meaningful. Always reward yourself as soon as possible after finishing each step. You have experienced enough delayed gratification in life. It's high time your mind saw a clear and unmistakable correlation between fulfilling goals and getting rewarded.

Stop being bad to yourself for not being good to yourself and start rewarding yourself for being good to yourself! Remember that whatever you think you are chasing is actually chasing you, just let go and it will catch up.

Expect Uneven Progress

Develop the conscious interrupt and learn to always observe yourself as we discussed in Chapter 15. Be clear about exactly what you want. Be bold. Be uncomfortable. Let go. Make your dreams real by defining and acting on your long- and short-term goals. Reward success. Keep at it and you will continue to alter the waveform to make what you want far more probable than it may be now by using the Law of Realization consciously.

Remember what we said in Chapter 16. You will probably notice your pace of change accelerating and seeming to move quickly and easily for some time. Then something will happen. Maybe you will fail to meet a step. Maybe it will seem like life is placing more and more demands on you as if trying to distract you. Your brain will cook up every imaginable excuse and circumstance to get you to turn back.

This is normal. This is your brain going into withdrawal because the old emotional cocktails have stopped moving through your veins. This is a good thing because it proves that your brain is doing all it can to follow its survival programming (core beliefs) to keep you alive. Honor and respect yourself for creating these obstacles. Look forward to the day when your brain keeps you in your ideal life with the same fervor.

Take smaller steps when this happens. Just keep moving forward no matter what. No excuses. Increase your rewards and take extra care not to punish yourself. Keep at it. Do not stop.

The obstacles will soon fade. You will find yourself making faster and faster progress. You will feel more confident and happy than you ever imagined. This will not be the fake desperate happiness of the Law of Attraction. This will be the deep satisfaction and self-love of the Law of Realization.

Keep it up.

You deserve nothing less.

* * *

Appendix A: Tools to Help You Succeed

The following books and audio programs expand on the topics contained in this book.

- *Through the Looking Glass: The Science behind The Law of Realization* by Anthony Hernandez and Jim Britt
- *Cracking the Rich Code* by Jim Britt
- *Cracking the Life Code* by Jim Britt
- *Cracking the Network Marketing Code* by Jim Britt
- *Do This. Get Rich! for Entrepreneurs* by Jim Britt
- *Do This. Get Rich! for Network Marketers* by Jim Britt
- *Rings of Truth* by Jim Britt
- *Unleashing Your Authentic Power* by Jim Britt
- *The Enlightened Savage* by Anthony Hernandez
- *The Natural Savage* by Anthony Hernandez
- *The Divine Savage* by Anthony Hernandez
- *The Romantic Savage* by Anthony Hernandez (coming 2013)
- *Small Business Success Secrets* by Anthony Hernandez
- *More Small Business Success Secrets* by Anthony Hernandez
- *Mrs. Ellingson's Amazing Quantum Classroom: Quantum Mechanics and More for Kids* by Anthony Hernandez (coming 2012)

* * *

Appendix B: Explorations in Science

This Appendix contains more insight into the science behind the Law of Realization. We originally had this material in Chapter 3 but moved it here because we wanted to focus the body of the book on explaining why the Law of Attraction does not work and what you can do about it. We created this Appendix because we find the science fascinating and hope you do too.

Please pick up a copy of *Through the Looking Glass: The Science Behind the Law of Realization* for a much deeper look at physics, the brain, and some of the amazing implications of what the science tells us.

The Hundred-Dollar Bill

Remember the hundred-dollar bill we talked about in Chapter 3? In that example, the odds of manifesting an additional atom are half the odds of manifesting the current number of atoms. This means that the odds of manifesting one atom are once in every two attempts, two atoms once in every four attempts, etc. The odds of manifesting all one hundred atoms are once in every 6.338×10^{29} attempts, or 1/2 multiplied by 1/2 one hundred times. That is 6.338 with twenty-six zeros after it. This is a very big number!

The universe is 13.7 billion years old. That adds up to 4.32×10^{17} seconds. If you started making one attempt to manifest a single hundred-dollar bill every second from the moment the Big Bang occurred, you would have to keep trying for 1.6 trillion times the current age of the universe before you could expect to succeed.

You would then have to manifest 9,999 more hundred-dollar bills to get your million dollars.

Keep in mind that this example assumes that each hundred-dollar bill consists of only one hundred atoms and that each atom has a fifty-fifty chance of being where and when you want it.

Actual hundred-dollar bills contain many trillions of atoms and the odds of manifesting a single atom are far less than fifty-fifty, which means you would need to wait countless trillions of times longer to get one hundred dollars. This is why the Law of Attraction is completely useless for any sort of practical purpose.

You can prove this for yourself very easily. Pretend that a coin controls each atom. If the coin comes up heads, the atom will appear where you want it to be. If the coin comes up tails, the atom will not appear where you want it to be. Flip a single coin and note that it comes up heads about once in every two flips. Add a second coin and you will notice that both come up heads about once in every four flips. Add a third coin and they all come up heads about once in every eight flips. Four coins will all come up heads about once every sixteen flips. The number of flips required for all coins to come up heads doubles with every new coin you add.

This is a great way to simulate the example we are using of an atom that cooperates with our wishes fifty percent of the time. Just because the atom cooperates with one attempt does not mean it will stay put or that it will cooperate with any future attempt. Each attempt must occur on its own merits because you will either manifest the hundred-dollar bill or not; you are not "growing" or "building" the bill atom by atom.

Interpreting Quantum Physics

The waveform that both allows and limits the Law of Attraction is the heart of heart of quantum physics. What does the waveform mean? Does quantum physics really prove the many claims made by self-help experts and others? Do quantum physics and relativity have anything to say about whether there is a higher power or intelligence in the universe? Maybe. It all depends on how one interprets the data.

Science agrees about the data from quantum physics. The debate is over how to interpret this data. The interpretation one chooses will shape how one sees the universe and our roles in it. This includes how one looks at concepts such as the Law of Attraction and the Universal Mind. There is nothing wrong with this so long as everyone remembers that a scientific interpretation is not the same thing as scientific proof. Keep that in mind as we take a look at the three main interpretations.

Copenhagen

The Copenhagen interpretation says that it is meaningless to ask what happens before the waveform collapses. The act of measuring creates or modifies reality by selecting one of the available possibilities based on the probability of each possible outcome.

Measuring devices like cameras and sensors cannot collapse the waveform because they are part of the experiment itself. For example, a camera records a waveform of an image that has a very high probability of displaying whatever you took the picture of. But what actually collapses that waveform?

Some scientists and philosophers say that collapse only happens when a conscious observer checks the results. This somewhat "far out" version of the Copenhagen interpretation can only mean that the observer creates the reality. Consciousness therefore influences—if not outright creates—matter. Small wonder that just about all self-help experts follow this interpretation. We subscribe to this interpretation and wrote this book accordingly. We did so with the full knowledge that many scientists consider it "far out." More on this a bit later.

If each of us creates our own reality in a universe where almost anything is possible then why isn't everybody living their ideal lives? Nobody wants to be poor, sick, hungry, isolated, unloved, or unhappy. Why is there so much misery in the world? Why can't people fly or live forever? Many bestselling books, movies, and other programs claim that we can have it if we can dream it. Are they wrong?

Yes and no. Each person does create her or his own reality but each person's reality can only exist within the laws of physics. For example, the laws of physics allow for the possibility that you can fly. These same laws also say that the probability of you being able to fly is very low. The laws of physics are a common framework that allows everyone to share her or his reality with everyone else. This framework limits us. Be glad the limits exist. Neither you nor the universe as we know it could exist without them.

If consciousness collapses the waveform then what happened before conscious life evolved? Maybe the universe evolved as a superposition of all possible universes until one of them evolved life. That first conscious being collapsed the waveform of the entire universe all the way back to the Big Bang that started it all.

Biocentrism (the theory that life created life) may explain why the universe seems so well suited to sustain life. This is not as crazy as it sounds because one cannot say that an observer creates reality while denying that the universe can exist without observers. Biocentrism also bridges the gap between creation and evolution because we can see that evolution is real without denying the Universal Mind that some call God.

Some flavors of the Copenhagen interpretation seem to directly involve consciousness. We can imagine a universe identical to ours without any life in it. We can also imagine a universe with living creatures that behave like robots without emotions, thoughts, feelings, or a sense of self. Consciousness and the sense of self have puzzled science for thousands of years.

Scientists have mapped the human brain and discovered mental circuits for many functions such as recognizing familiar faces or focusing our attention. We know much about how the brain works but all of our searching has not revealed where "we" live inside our heads. Many scientists therefore choose to avoid the entire problem. Some of them even devise interpretations that try to get around consciousness.

Hidden Variables

The hidden variables interpretation tries to avoid consciousness by saying that there is a deeper level of reality. Objects in this interpretation do not exist in superposition. They have real positions and speeds whether or not someone measures them. The fact that we cannot detect all of these values has nothing to do with the universe and everything to do with our own limitations. Objective reality does exist. We just can't see it.

This interpretation has several serious problems. Experiments have proven that nonlocality is real and demonstrated that objective reality does not exist. Adding hidden variables does nothing to improve quantum physics. All it does is gum up the math. Quantum physics works just fine without these variables. We can therefore safely guess that there are no hidden variables. This attempt to bypass consciousness does not seem to work at all. This leaves us with either Copenhagen or many-worlds.

Many Worlds

The many-worlds interpretation says that our universe splits into multiple copies every time a quantum event happens. This avoids the waveform and collapse and bypasses consciousness. For example, a coin toss splits the universe into two copies. The coin comes up heads in one copy and tails in the other. Throwing a die splits the universe into six copies. Throwing two dice splits the universe into thirty six copies. You get the idea.

Splits happen every time some A or B possibility opens up anywhere in the universe. Each of the resulting copies splits when something happens over there. Those new copies keep splitting and the total number of universes soon runs into the trillions. You yourself split into copies and copies of copies. Your own death is an event with a probability. You end up dead in many trillions of universes. You also end up living forever in just as many different universes.

This interpretation is a great way to avoid dealing with consciousness. It is also a very inefficient theory that cannot be tested. Science dislikes theories that cannot be tested.

This seems to leave us with the Copenhagen interpretation as the best possible choice. It seems that consciousness may play a central role in the universe. The concept of a Universal Mind may not be as crazy or "far out" as it sounds even though many mainstream scientists might beg to differ.

It's All Relative

What about the Universal Mind, cosmic consciousness, or higher power that some self-help experts say we can tap into? We need to leave the world of the very small and travel to the world of the very large to answer this question. We need to look at Albert Einstein's theories of relativity.

Our sense of time depends on how fast we are moving compared to the speed of light. Different observers moving at different speeds may measure different distances, elapsed times, and even different sequences of events. For example, Observer A may see two events happening at the same time while Observer B sees them happening at different times. Each observer takes her or his own private path through space-time.

Imagine two identical twins who are born at the exact same moment and who will lead identical life spans with both of them dying precisely at midnight on their 80th birthdays. Twin A remains on Earth while Twin B accelerates to eighty percent of light speed for his entire life. Both twins experience 80 years of life that seem to pass by at the same speed for each of them. Twin

B returns to Earth one minute before his death. Imagine his surprise when he learns that one hundred and thirty six years have passed on Earth and that Twin A has been dead for fifty-six years!

This only makes sense if we stop seeing space and time as separate things. We need to see time as a fourth dimension that unites with our familiar three-dimensions of length, height, and width. Relativity tells us that space and time are a single geometric thing called space-time. Nature balances out the fifty-six year difference by changing the space that Twin B traveled through. Twins A and B therefore experience the exact same amount of space-time. This is only possible if space (S) and time (T) are one and the same. We experience them as separate but this is merely a very convincing illusion.

The next step is to unite mass and energy. The famous equation $e=mc^2$ means that energy (E) and mass (M) are the same and that one can change into the other. Mass increases with speed and reaches infinity at light speed. A car speeding down the highway weighs more than the same car parked in the garage. Mass causes gravity by bending space-time. Mass also increases as speed increases.

Relativity unites matter with energy, space with time, and mass with gravity. We can also unify space and gravity because gravity is nothing more than bent space-time. This leads us to the conclusion that space (S) equals time (T) equals energy (E) equals mass (M), or that S=T=E=M.

You may be wondering just what this has to do with the Law of Attraction, the Law of Realization, or the Universal Mind. It turns out that the total amount of energy in the universe adds up to…

… Wait for it…

… Zero!

You read that correctly. There is zero total energy in the universe. S=T=E=M=0. Zip. Zero. Zilch. The entire universe adds up to one giant nothing.

How can we make sense of this? What does any of this have to do with any sort of higher power or intelligence? How can you use this information to make positive changes in your life? These are great questions. Let's find out.

The Universal Mind

The Secret says that, "Physicists tell us that the entire Universe emerged from thought!" John Hagelin says that, "Quantum physics and quantum cosmology confirm that the universe essentially emerges from thought and that all of the matter around us is just precipitated thought."

The belief that mind creates matter is called *idealism*. If idealism is correct then consciousness and the thoughts that consciousness generates really are the stuff of which the universe is made. This consciousness is what *The Secret* calls the Universal Mind and what people often refer to as God or a "higher power." The Universal Mind is, "the attractive force which brings electrons together by the 'Law of Attraction' so they form atoms; the atoms brought together to create molecules..."

Thomas Troward was a leading New Thought thinker in the nineteenth century. He said that thought comes before physical things and that, "the action of Mind plants that nucleus which, if allowed to grow undisturbed, will eventually attract to itself all the conditions necessary for its manifestation in outward visible form." Mystic Meher Baba put it far more simply when he said, "Don't worry. Be happy."

Does this mean that, "Nothing can come into your experience unless you summon it through persistent thoughts." as *The Secret* claims? Does this mean that, "We are unlimited beings. We have no ceiling, The capabilities and the gifts and the power that is within every single individual on the planet is unlimited." as Bernard Beckwith says?

Not really. Some physicists and philosophers believe that quantum physics proves idealism. They could be right. Then again, mainstream science considers idealism to be "far out." Most scientists believe that matter creates mind. This model of reality is called *materialism* and is the opposite of idealism.

Many religious people believe that the physical and spiritual worlds are both real. This is called *dualism*. Dualism cannot be true because it violates the basic laws of physics having to do with energy transfer. Please see *The Divine Savage* by Anthony for more information on materialism, dualism, idealism, and the nature of reality.

Finding the Universal Mind

An old proverb tells of two monks arguing about a flag flapping in the wind. The first monk insists that the flag is moving. The second insists that the wind is moving. A third monk walks by and says, "Your minds are moving!"

Idealism says that the Universal Mind is the ultimate foundation of the universe. If this is correct then everything in the universe is part of the Universal Mind and the appearance of separate objects is an illusion. The idea that you, Jim Britt, Anthony Hernandez, and everyone else are separate beings is part of this illusion.

When you dream, your mind creates a complete universe with space, time, energy, matter, and other people. You see yourself as a separate object and interact with everything in your dream as separate objects. Wake up in the morning and you immediately know that all of the people, places, and things in your dream all existed inside your one brain. You see the illusion for what it is. What we see as the waking world could be another layer of dreaming.

Two plus three equals three plus two in the normal world but we cannot say the same thing about quantum experiments. Consciousness seems to play a role in quantum experiments because the results often depend on how the experiment is set up. This is one example of creating our own reality through our thoughts, feelings, and beliefs. Let's examine this idea using the "far out" version of the Copenhagen interpretation we saw earlier.

Only consciousness and possibility exist before a measurement. The waveform carries every possible outcome. Measurement selects one of the possibilities as the reality. This creates both the result and the illusion of separation. The Earth is not the center of the universe. Each of us is a center.

We are not talking about "attraction" or "manifesting" here. Collapse is much more subtle and limited than that. The wave function obeys the laws of physics and limits the possible outcomes. Consciousness also obeys the laws of quantum physics. This is why the Law of Attraction is useless by itself. This also points the way to the far more powerful tool that we can use to improve our lives that we call consciously using the Law of Realization.

If idealism is correct then particles are part of atoms that are part of molecules that are part of cells that are part of tissues that are part of organs that are part of living beings that are part of self-awareness that is part of consciousness. Consciousness explains itself and everything else. Materialism and dualism strip life of meaning and destroy freedom of will. Idealism gives life both freedom and meaning.

Waveforms work both forward and backward in time. Time itself is an illusion caused by the string of measurement and collapses that gives us the sensation of time. Think of every instant of time as a stepping stone. Hopping from one stone to the next gives us the feeling of time but the stones themselves always exist. We could circle back to a stone that we visited before but would not perceive it as going back in time.

If this interpretation is correct then consciousness must be nonlocal in order to collapse a nonlocal waveform. That could have powerful implications for the idea of a Universal Mind. In this model, part of our consciousness exists in local reality. This is the part we see as Anthony, Jim, you, or anyone else. The other part of our consciousness lives as one with everything and everyone in the universe. The unified portions of our consciousness collapse the waveform. Twenty people witnessing the same event will see that event differently. These different perceptions are all part of the same waveform.

Idealism says that space, time, energy, and matter are all consciousness. Consciousness itself is nothing, as in "no thing" because it not tangible or measurable. This is why science cannot find it inside our heads. Consciousness is also everything. It is the absolute and unchanging intelligence that functions in an eternal present and provides the ultimate source of experience. Matter is made of collapsed waveforms. Waveforms contain all possible forms or designs that collapse into a single manifestation. We could say that the waveform itself is the design.

The idea of consciousness being nothing fits with the equation S=T=E=M=0 that we showed you in the previous chapter. How can existence be real if everything is nothing? Contradictory items often imply each other. The idea of nothing can imply the idea of something and vice-versa. Think of space as a mathematical set. A set by itself is both real and empty unless filled. This concept lets us think of the universe as both nothing and everything.

We cannot have existence (individual fragments or pieces) without nonexistence (the whole). The form of any given unit is a spatial aspect of that unit's nothingness. Nothingness explains itself as pure consciousness.

If consciousness creates the universe and everything in it then consciousness itself is the Universal Mind that some call God. This Universal Mind is very powerful but is not all-powerful because the laws of physics limit how it creates experience. The Universal Mind shattered itself into many pieces like a mirror dropped on the floor. Each shard of that mirror is part of the whole mirror. Each of us is a shard of the Universal Mind.

Materialism dominates science and sees idealism as "far out" in the best of cases. This is perfectly natural. We only see matter and feel energy. Our minds are so good at creating the physical universe that we almost never stop to ask questions. Most of the questions we do ask are theoretical. There is nothing wrong with looking for mind and Universal Mind in our genes or brains. There is nothing wrong with performing quantum experiments.

We can imagine a universe just like ours where consciousness does not exist. Consciousness therefore exists over and above physical facts no matter which interpretation one uses. A purely material universe does not need consciousness but here it is. There is no way to get around the fact that what we see as reality is the end of a process that involves consciousness. We believe a world exists "out there" beyond our senses but everything we perceive, think, and feel is inside our heads.

Is it more amazing to say than an eternal consciousness created the universe as a sort of dream or that the universe simply popped into being by itself? That, dear reader, is up to you.

Which Interpretation is Correct?

Belief matters a lot less than you think. We believe that the consciousness-based flavor of the Copenhagen interpretation combined with the idealist model of reality is the only approach that fits and explains the data from quantum physics, relativity, and other sciences and theories... but we could be wrong.

Mainstream science does not accept this model. Most scientists consider most of the information in this book to be "far out." Some may even see it as dead wrong. Your own model of reality may or may not allow for concepts such as the Law of Attraction and the Universal Mind.

We can tell you for a fact that quantum physics does not prove that we can manifest anything we want. It cannot do any such thing because it only deals in probability and not actuality. All quantum physics can tell you is the odds of something happening at a given time and place.

Brain science does not prove that we can access any sort of Universal Mind or higher power. Anyone who makes claims like these is either misinformed or up to no good or both.

Mainstream science does accept the quantum waveform. Waveforms do indeed mean that just about anything is possible. We can therefore say that the Law of Attraction is technically real.

The same waveform also says that the odds of actually using the Law of Attraction as advertised in *The Secret* and other popular programs are astronomically low unless you have billions or even trillions of years on your hands. The model we present in this book is therefore accurate for practical purposes no matter which interpretation or model of reality one subscribes to.

This book described a way to improve your life and get what you want regardless of what you believe and how you see reality. We are confident that most mainstream scientists will agree with our method. A few of these scientists may not like how we explain this method but we hope and believe that even they will admit that it has merit.

We see this book and the waveform collapse that we call the Law of Realization as the missing ingredient to the Law of Attraction. It does not matter if you believe us or not. All you have to do is use the Law of Realization to consciously affect the waveforms in your life and it will work no matter which interpretation of quantum mechanics you prefer.

We happen to be idealists who believe that mind creates matter in accordance with the laws of physics as seen through the

Copenhagen interpretation. We believe that space, time, energy, and matter are all illusions. We believe that consciousness is the factory that creates the universe. It is the engine that powers the universe. It is the measurement that collapses the waveform. It is the nothingness in the great emptiness that is everything.

Again, you don't have to believe us. You may see the universe completely differently than we do. It does not matter. Consciousness always exists in the present no matter how you look at it. The present time is all there is. There is no past or future. Neither exists. It is always now.

Recalling an experience from the past does nothing more than evoke a psychological response in the present. The strength of your present experience depends on how vivid your recollection is based on how that experience impacted you.

Hanging on to a past experience can produce the same physical and emotional response that occurred when the event first happened. The event is not happening to us now and yet our reaction can be very much the same. It can even be stronger because of the suppressed energy we are carrying.

Recalling an unpleasant experience drains our energy and makes us tense, depressed, or unhappy. Recalling pleasant experiences tends to make us feel happy. Take a moment to recall a past experience that made you feel sad, angry, or unhappy. Notice how that makes you feel now. Now think of something joyful from your past.

You will notice two things. First, you'll notice how difficult it was to switch from being unhappy to being happy. Second, you'll notice how the experience of joy uplifts you once you make the switch. All you had to do is observe the unwanted emotion and then let it go like a piece of garbage you toss in the trash can. This works no matter how you interpret reality or what you believe.

Appendix C: About the Authors

Jim Britt

Jim Britt is an entrepreneur, author, speaker, and peak performance specialist, a noted success advisor, and an internationally recognized leader in the field of personal empowerment and peak performance training.

Jim has authored sixteen books and programs including *Rings of Truth, The Power of Letting Go, Unleashing Your Authentic Power, Cracking the Rich Code,* and *Do This. Get Rich! for Entrepreneurs.*

Based on years of research and personal application, Jim offers a unique blend of ancient truths and practical modern applications to deliver a soul-stirring message of personal transformation.

Jim Britt's message is guaranteed to move you regardless of your background, education, or experience. Whether you are a reader of one of Jim's books or a workshop participant, it will be an indescribable, thought provoking, emotional journey that will lead you to self-discovery and personal change. Jim's unique combination of personal style and message content impacts everyone. He will ignite your imagination for becoming all you can be.

Jim has presented seminars and workshops to thousands of audiences totaling over 1,000,000 people from all walks of life. Jim's "letting go" processes provide specific tools that eliminate unwanted feelings, emotions, and outdated beliefs that block success and happiness. Jim also provides hand-on strategies for increasing one' s performance, success, and personal wealth to entrepreneurs and success seekers.

Jim leverages his skills and experience as one of the leading experts in peak performance, entrepreneurship, and personal empowerment coaching and training to produce stellar results. He was recently named one of the top 20 living success coaches, and presented with the "Best of the Best" award out of the top 100 contributors of all time to the direct selling industry.

For more information or to book Jim as a keynote speaker for your next special event, please visit:www.JimBritt.com.

Email inquiries should be sent to: support@jimbritt.com

Anthony Hernandez

Anthony Hernandez is an entrepreneur, coach, author, and speaker in the fields of small business marketing/management and personal empowerment. He has authored over 200 technical manuals, 150 articles, and 12 books including *Small Business Success Secrets, More Small Business Success Secrets, The Enlightened Savage, The Natural Savage,* and *The Divine Savage.* His next book, due in 2013, is *The Romantic Savage.*

Anthony has devoted years to the study of quantum mechanics, relativity, evolution, philosophy, religion, and spirituality. His research for the Savage series led him to the conclusion that the Law of Attraction cannot work as intended. This discovery led to the book you are now holding in your hands.

Audiences of all ages from elementary school children to adults from all walks of life enjoy Anthony's presentations and easy conversational style that make complex technical and scientific information understandable without ever dumbing it down. Anthony explains how the universe works and how our built-in limitations can lead us to the success we all want and deserve.

Anthony is also a founding member and the Chief Marketing Officer for The Community Link (www.thecommunitylink.net), which leverages the latest technologies to empower local communities and strengthen local economies by paying customers to shop local. The Community Link also actively supports local schools and other nonprofits by offering active and passive fund-raising channels. Please visit The Community Link to learn how you can earn residual income by helping your local community thrive.

For more information or to book Anthony as a keynote for your next special event, please visit:www.CoachAnthony.com.

Email inquiries should be sent to: anthony@coachanthony.com

* * *

CPSIA information can be obtained at www.ICGtesting.com
Printed in the USA
LVOW132208120613

338357LV00001B/115/P

9 780966 217117